KGQ005F

Population Aging
in the
United States

Recent Titles in
Contributions to the Study of Aging

Public Policy Opinion and the Elderly, 1952-1978
John E. Tropman

The Mirror of Time: Images of Aging and Dying
Joan M. Boyle and James E. Morriss

North American Elders: United States and Canadian Perspectives
Eloise Rathbone-McCuan and Betty Havens, editors

Hispanic Elderly in Transition: Theory, Research, Policy and Practice
Steven R. Applewhite, editor

Religion, Health, and Aging: A Review and Theoretical Integration
Harold George Koenig, Mona Smiley, and Jo Ann Ploch Gonzales

Philanthropy and Gerontology: The Role of American Foundations
Ann H. L. Sontz

Perceptions of Aging in Literature: A Cross-Cultural Study
Prisca von Dorotka Bagnell and Patricia Spencer Soper, editors

Residential Care for the Elderly: Critical Issues in Public Policy
Sharon A. Baggett

Senior Centers in America
John A. Krout

Shared Housing for the Elderly
Dale J. Jaffe, editor

Who Cares for Them? Workers in the Home Care Industry
Penny Hollander Feldman with Alice M. Sapienza and Nancy M. Kane

Aiding and Aging: The Coming Crisis in Support for the Elderly
by Kin and State
John Mogey, editor

Population Aging in the United States

William J. Serow,
David F. Sly,
   and
J. Michael Wrigley

Contributions to the Study of Aging, Number 18
ERDMAN B. PALMORE, *Series Adviser*

Greenwood Press
New York • Westport, Connecticut • London

Library of Congress Cataloging-in-Publication Data

Serow, William J.
  Population aging in the United States / William J. Serow, David F.
Sly, and J. Michael Wrigley.
    p. cm. — (Contributions to the study of aging, ISSN
0732-085X ; no. 18)
  Includes bibliographical references.
  ISBN 0-313-27311-1 (lib. bdg. : alk. paper)
  1. Aged—United States. 2. Age distribution (Demography)—United
States. 3. United States—Population. I. Sly, David F.
II. Wrigley, J. Michael. III. Title. IV. Series.
HQ1064.U5S467 1990
305.26'0973—dc20   89-25699

British Library Cataloguing in Publication Data is available.

Library of Congress Catalog Card Number: 89-25699
ISBN: 0-313-27311-1
ISSN: 0732-085X

First published in 1990

Greenwood Press, 88 Post Road West, Westport, Connecticut 06881
An imprint of Greenwood Publishing Group, Inc.

Printed in the United States of America

The paper used in this book complies with the
Permanent Paper Standard issued by the National
Information Standards Organization (Z39.48-1984).

10 9 8 7 6 5 4 3 2 1

CONTENTS

ILLUSTRATIONS

FIGURES

TABLES

Introduction

The purpose of this book is to review some of the more salient aspects of the demographic, social, and economic aspects of the aging of the population of the United States. Although the aging of individuals clearly begins at the moment of birth, the aging of populations can be defined as the increase in both numbers and proportions of the total population of persons at and above some chronologically defined point. This point is arbitrary and should not necessarily be taken as indicative of biological changes that are occurring to all individuals at that point in their life. While from several perspectives it might be appropriate to discuss the determinants and consequences of biological aging, the availability of requisite demographic, social, and economic data requires the choice of some chronologically defined age as the focus. Although arguments could be developed to justify any one of several ages as defining the lower boundary of "the older population," we simply assert that for our purposes this boundary is set at age 60.

As has been well established in the demographic literature, the current age structure of any population is the consequence of prior levels of fertility, mortality, and (to a varying extent) migration (Coale, 1972; Keyfitz, 1968). The number of older individuals in a population at any time is a direct reflection of the number of births occurring in that population sixty or more years

ago, the levels of mortality to which those births have been ex-
posed during their entire lifetime, and the levels of migration-
related increments or decrements to those cohorts that currently
comprise the older population. The share of older individuals in a
population at any time is a direct reflection of both their numbers
as well as the number of persons at all younger ages. The latter, of
course, simply reflects the number of births that have occurred
over the most recent fifty-nine years and the mortality and migration experiences of these cohorts. Future trends in the aging of a
population will accordingly reflect prospective levels of fertility,
mortality, and migration.

This book begins with a retrospective review of the population
aging process of the United States throughout the twentieth century and continues with a prospective view of aging through most
of the next century. In order to establish the overall context
within which the aging process of the American population is
occurring, chapter 1 begins with a cursory overview of population
aging throughout the world. This chapter then goes on to deal
with trends in numbers of older persons and the share of the total
population represented by those aged 60 and over. It considers
age composition from the perspective both of the older population
relative to the population as a whole and of the structural change
within the older population itself. Although age is the fundamental
axis of disaggregation here, attention is paid to the axes of gender
and race. In terms of consideration of the future course of aging,
current projections of the age-race-gender structure of the U.S.
population, as prepared by the Bureau of the Census (Spencer,
1989), are introduced.

Chapter 2 considers the demographic determinants of population aging and examines the roles that each of the three demographic processes has actually played in shaping the status quo, as
well as the roles that they may play into the future. In this context,
a considerable amount of attention is devoted to the role that
future mortality variations play in determining the size and structure of the older population. This concentration on mortality arises
from the simple fact that future levels of fertility will have no
influence upon the absolute size or structure of the older population until midway through the twenty-first century. While future
levels and structures of immigration will play some short-run role
in this population's size and composition, in all probability the
influence of this variable will be dwarfed by the role of variations

in mortality among those already enumerated among the American population.

Chapter 3 deals with the spatial aspects of aging in the United States. At the national level, we need pay only modest attention to the role that migration has played and will play in the aging of the population. At the subnational level, though, migration or the redistribution of the population becomes the critical variable in the determination of differences in levels and patterns of aging. This chapter focuses first on changing patterns of distribution of the older population in terms of urban-rural and metropolitan-non-metropolitan residence, as well as on patterns for regions within the nation. Second, the chapter treats the question of the role that migration and residential mobility have played and are likely to play on redistribution of the older population, including the comparative importance of migration and aging in place. The chapter also considers the emerging evidence on the variability of migration patterns among the elderly by age and the redistributive consequences of this variability.

The next three chapters deal with various social and economic aspects of aging and of the older population in the United States. Chapter 4 treats the marital status, living arrangements, and actual housing characteristics of the older population. The discussion on marital status concentrates largely on changing proportions who are currently married versus widowed, although some attention is also paid to the rising incidence of divorced persons, especially among the younger elderly. Closely related to although conceptually different from this concept are living arrangements, that is, a consideration of the structure of the households in which older persons live. Critical to this discussion is the greater tendency of older persons to live in their own household (alone or with spouse) or in an institution and the offsetting reduction in the tendency to share a household with non-spousal relatives, especially children. Finally, the chapter briefly considers the characteristics of the housing units occupied by older households in terms of their size, ownership, and availability of amenities.

Chapter 5 deals with the economic characteristics of previous, current, and future generations of older Americans. This chapter treats three general issues: labor force, income, and educational attainment. Under the rubric of labor force, the chapter considers recent trends in labor force participation among the older population. Because these are very much a function of eligibility for retirement programs, the chapter also includes a brief review of recent legislative changes governing compulsory retirement and the age of eligibility for partial and full Social Security retirement benefits. The discussion of labor force participation also includes differences by gender and the difference between part-time versus full-time labor force attachment. Additionally, there is some consideration of the occupational and industrial structure of the older work force.

The discussion of income levels concentrates on age and gender differentials within the older population and pays close attention to the role that various sources of income play in determining the comparative economic well-being of segments of the older population. Inasmuch as the access to a source of income other than Social Security and survivors' benefits (especially a private or governmental service pension) has a great deal of influence on comparative well-being (Kotlikoff and Smith, 1983), these differences in income sources come under particularly close scrutiny. This portion of the chapter also considers the difference between individual and household income levels for the older population. Finally, there is some consideration of the observed differences in patterns of consumer expenditures between the younger and older segments of the population and within the older population itself.

The final section of this chapter discusses the question of the educational attainment of the older population. For historic reasons, the older component of the population has long lagged behind the balance in terms of educational attainment. This gap will be closing in the future as the older population during the next century increasingly comes to include persons who were born after the end of World War II and whose educational attainment has been much greater than that of older cohorts, but not appreciably less than that of more recent cohorts.

Chapter 6 addresses the critical issue of health. Health status and health care access and utilization are perhaps the single most critical aspect of an aging population, and the economic implications for funding this care are profound. This chapter reviews data on morbidity and disability as well as patterns of the utilization of health care facilities, including the demand for nursing home or other long-term care. Particular attention is paid here to the relationship between mortality levels and trends, on the one hand, and levels and incidences of morbidity and disability on the other.

Chapter 7 of the book considers the policy implications of the aging of the U.S. population. To a not inconsiderable extent, policy discussions pervade much of the material that has gone before. In this chapter, we synthesize the policy ramifications of changes in the size and composition of the older population, with particular emphasis on the demand for health care and the economic well-being of older individuals. Associated with these ramifications are other policy considerations regarding inter-generational relationships both within families and for society as a whole.

Trends in Population Aging

The first task in discussing population aging within the United States should be to place the process of aging in this country in the context of population aging as it is occurring throughout the world. The relative extent and tempo of population aging in the United States are illustrated by the summary data included in appendix 1, which presents statistical tables from the recent U.S. Bureau of the Census publication *An Aging World* (Torrey, Kinsella, and Taeuber, 1987). These data establish that, at present, the level of aging in the United States is slightly behind that occurring in western Europe, but generally more advanced than that which has hitherto occurred elsewhere in Europe or in other developed societies in North America, Oceania, or Asia. The United States has, of course, experienced more aging in recent years than was the case for a representative sample of developing nations. Over the course of time, aging in the United States is likely to occur at a somewhat greater pace than in most other developed nations. Prospective growth rates for both the older population as a whole as well as for each age group that comprises this subpopulation are likely to exceed those of other developed nations except Japan from the present until the year 2005 and to exceed those of all developed nations with the exception of New Zealand and Japan (only at ages 75 and over) through the year 2025. Conversely, the rate of population aging in the sample of developing nations included in appendix 1 is likely to exceed that of the United States or any other developed nation to a substantial and generally increasing extent.

Table 1.1 presents the historical record of the growth of the older population in the United States during the twentieth century, as well as current projections prepared by the U.S. Bureau of the Census (Spencer, 1989). The projections shown here are the so-called midrange projections, which assume (a) that the ultimate level of completed fertility will be 1.8; (b) that life expectation at birth will rise from base year (1986) levels of 71.5 for males and 78.5 for females to 77.8 and 84.7 years, respectively, by the year 2080; and (c) that net immigration will total some 500 thousand persons per year, with age-gender-race composition based upon that observed in the mid-1980s.

The top panel shows the number of persons (in thousands) in each five-year age group at ten-year intervals from 1900 to 2080, the terminal year for which projections are currently available. During the period from 1900 to 1980, the total population of the United States tripled, from 76 to 227 million persons. At the same time, the older population expanded by a factor of seven from 5 to 36 million persons. Finally, during this perod, the very old population, aged 85 or more years, increased by a factor of nearly twenty, from 120 thousand to more than 2 million persons. As a consequence of the relatively greater rates of growth observed among persons aged 60 + and among persons aged 85 + , the share of the total population accounted for by these age groups rose from 6.4 and 0.2 percent, respectively, in 1900 to 15.7 and 1.0 percent in 1980.

Patterns of change for each age group within the older population are shown in the second panel of table 1.1. These data show actual and projected rates of change for each of the six thirty-year periods that exhaust the 1900-2080 period. Two important observations may be made from these data. First, not only does the growth rate of the elderly population exceed that for the total in each period (in fact, the elderly growth rate is at least twice that of the total except for the earliest period), but the relative difference between growth rates tends to widen over time. This observation is especially true for the future, when the growth rate of the elderly is about four times that of the total from 1990 to 2020 and about ten times greater from 2020 to 2050. After the year 2040, absolute population decline sets in for the entire population, while

Table 1.1
Older Population of the United States, by Age, 1900-2080 (thousands of persons)

Year	60-64	65-69	70-74	75-79	80-84	85+	65+	Total	Percent 60+	Percent 85+
1900	1,795	1,304	885	520	252	123	4,879	75,994	6.4%	.2%
1910	2,271	1,682	1,115	668	322	168	6,226	92,059	6.8%	.2%
1920	2,989	2,072	1,397	857	403	211	7,929	105,872	7.5%	.2%
1930	3,760	2,776	1,953	1,108	535	272	10,404	123,108	8.5%	.2%
1940	4,740	3,815	2,574	1,506	775	365	13,775	132,165	10.4%	.3%
1950	6,074	5,013	3,419	2,156	1,128	578	18,368	151,326	12.1%	.4%
1960	7,142	6,258	4,739	3,054	1,580	929	23,702	179,323	13.2%	.5%
1970	8,617	6,992	5,444	3,835	2,284	1,511	28,683	203,212	14.1%	.7%
1980	10,088	8,782	6,798	4,794	2,935	2,240	35,637	226,546	15.7%	1.0%
1990	10,741	10,251	8,122	6,105	3,828	3,254	42,301	250,410	16.9%	1.3%
2000	10,699	9,491	8,752	7,282	4,735	4,622	45,581	268,266	17.0%	1.7%
2010	16,171	12,163	8,876	6,913	5,295	6,115	55,533	282,575	19.7%	2.2%
2020	20,276	17,467	13,506	8,981	5,462	6,651	72,343	294,364	24.6%	2.3%
2030	17,675	18,958	17,030	13,023	8,464	8,129	83,279	300,629	27.7%	2.7%
2040	16,729	15,843	14,965	14,260	10,790	12,251	84,838	301,807	28.1%	4.1%
2050	18,425	17,325	14,265	12,042	9,613	15,287	86,957	299,849	29.0%	5.1%
2060	17,131	17,185	15,803	13,334	9,308	14,641	87,402	296,963	29.4%	4.9%
2070	17,222	16,310	14,802	13,359	10,447	15,506	87,646	294,642	29.7%	5.3%
2080	17,481	16,951	14,977	12,820	9,917	16,966	89,112	292,235	30.5%	5.8%

Table 1.1 (continued)

Percent Change

	60-64	65-69	70-74	75-79	80-84	85+	60+	Total
1900-1930	109.5%	112.9%	120.7%	113.1%	112.3%	121.1%	113.2%	62.0%
1930-1960	89.9%	125.4%	142.7%	175.6%	195.3%	241.5%	127.8%	45.7%
1960-1990	50.4%	63.8%	71.4%	99.9%	142.3%	250.3%	78.5%	39.6%
1990-2020	88.8%	70.4%	66.3%	47.1%	42.7%	104.4%	71.0%	17.6%
2020-2050	-9.1%	-.8%	5.6%	34.1%	76.0%	129.8%	20.2%	1.9%
2050-2080	-5.1%	-2.2%	5.0%	6.5%	3.2%	11.0%	2.5%	-2.5%

Percent of Older Population

	60-64	65-69	70-74	75-79	80-84	85+
1900	36.8%	26.7%	18.1%	10.7%	5.2%	2.5%
1910	36.5%	27.0%	17.9%	10.7%	5.2%	2.7%
1920	37.7%	26.1%	17.6%	10.8%	5.1%	2.7%
1930	36.1%	26.7%	18.8%	10.6%	5.1%	2.6%
1940	34.4%	27.7%	18.7%	10.9%	5.6%	2.6%

Year						
1950	33.1%	27.3%	18.6%	11.7%	6.1%	3.1%
1960	30.1%	26.4%	20.0%	12.9%	6.7%	3.9%
1970	30.0%	24.4%	19.0%	13.4%	8.0%	5.3%
1980	28.3%	24.6%	19.1%	13.5%	8.2%	6.3%
1990	25.4%	24.2%	19.2%	14.4%	9.0%	7.7%
2000	23.5%	20.8%	19.2%	16.0%	10.4%	10.1%
2010	29.1%	21.9%	16.0%	12.4%	9.5%	11.0%
2020	28.0%	24.1%	18.7%	12.4%	7.6%	9.2%
2030	21.2%	22.8%	20.4%	15.6%	10.2%	9.8%
2040	19.7%	18.7%	17.6%	16.8%	12.7%	14.4%
2050	21.2%	19.9%	16.4%	13.8%	11.1%	17.6%
2060	19.6%	19.7%	18.1%	15.3%	10.6%	16.8%
2070	19.6%	18.6%	16.9%	15.2%	11.9%	17.7%
2080	19.6%	19.0%	16.8%	14.4%	11.1%	19.0%

Sources: Decennial Censuses of Population: 1900-1980; Spencer, 1989, p. 38-105

5

the older population continues to expand, albeit at historically low rates. Second, as a general rule, it is the case that the older the five-year age group in question, the greater is the rate of growth. This fact is almost uniformly true for all periods after 1930, with the exception of the period from 1990 to 2020, when we see those persons born during the peak years of the "baby boom" in the late 1950s attaining the age of 60. Even during this period, the growth rate among the very old population surpasses that of the 60-64 age group.

The consequences of the patterns of growth rate differentials are displayed in the bottom panel of the table, which shows for each year the proportion of the total older population accounted for by each individual age group. In 1900, almost two-thirds of the older population was under age 70, and only 8 percent was over age 80. At present, only about half the older population is under 70, and about 17 percent is at least 80 years old. By the end of the projection period, only about 40 percent of the older population would be aged 60-69, and 30 percent or more would be 80 and over.

Some of the distributional aspects of growth and change in the older population of the United States are illustrated in table 1.2, which explores some ratios in age structure, as well as gender and racial composition of the older population for selected years between 1900 and 2080. The uppermost panel shows various population age ratios for the older population relative to other age groups and within the older population itself. The first three lines depict the conventional dependency ratio, showing the numbers of youth (0-19), the elderly, and all "dependents" relative to the absolute size of the working-age population. The third line shows remarkably little variation in dependency over the nearly two hundred year period, with the ratio ranging from as little as 0.8 (in both 1940 and 2000) to nearly 1.1 (in both 1960 and 2080). What is perhaps most striking about the dependency ratio (other than its overall stability) is the compositional change in that portion of the population that is not of working age. In the early years of the present century there were six children for every older person; in the middle of the century, the ratio declined to 3 to 1 and stands now about 2 to 1. Since the projected population of the twenty-first century begins to decline, the youth dependency ratio remains quite fixed throughout the century, while that of the elderly continues to rise. After 2020, there are more persons aged 60+ than aged 0-19 in the population, although only in the ratio of 1.2-1.4 to 1.

The fourth line in table 1.2 displays the ratio of persons currently aged 60 to 69 years old to those currently aged 85 or more years old. In a general sense, these data might be interpreted as representing the relative size of successive generations within the older population. As a result of observed and prospective changes in age-specific mortality within the older population (a topic to be considered in depth in chapter 2), there is likely to be an increased incidence of two generations of older persons alive within the same family. As can be seen in table 1.2, the ratio of "young old" to "oldest old" has declined rapidly since 1940 to the present (from more than 20 to 1 to about 8 to 1) and is likely to decline by more than half again in the short period to the end of the century. Thereafter (discounting the temporary increase in 2020, once again because of the aging of the baby boom cohorts), this ratio declines gradually to a terminal level of about 2 to 1.

The fifth line in table 1.2 shows a similar ratio in what might be viewed as the opposite direction, namely the ratio of the young old to an age group that is likely to be their children (chosen for illustrative purposes as persons aged 45 to 49). Historically, this ratio has increased considerably during the present century from levels slightly above unity in 1900 and 1920 to a current level of 2.3, owing largely to mortality reductions at the older ages. Unlike the preceding ratio, however, this ratio changes only slightly after 1980 (except for a temporary reduction in 2000 followed by a temporary upsurge in 2020, when the large birth cohorts of the 1950s attain the ages of 45-49 and 60-69) until the very end of the projection period, when the terminal level of 2.8 is reached.

The second panel of data shows the proportion of the entire older population that has been or that is projected to be nonwhite. Although the U.S. population as a whole has become increasingly nonwhite in recent years (because of sustained fertility differentials and, more recently, an increased share of nonwhites among the immigrant population) it is only quite recently that this phenomenon has begun to occur within the older population. This phenomenon is the consequence of the pronounced differences in mortality between racial groups, especially at the younger ages. In the future, the racial structure of the older population is likely to

Table 1.2
Selected Demographic Indicators for the Population Aged 60 and Over, United States,
1900-2080

	1900	1920	1940	1960	1980	2000	2020	2040	2060	2080
Ratios of Age groups:										
0-19 to 20-59	.90	.79	.62	.79	.61	.49	.46	.45	.45	.45
60+ to 20-59	.13	.14	.19	.27	.30	.31	.48	.57	.61	.64
0-19 and 60+ to 20-59	1.03	.93	.81	1.07	.91	.80	.94	1.02	1.06	1.09
60-69 to 85+	25.29	24.01	23.40	14.42	8.42	4.07	5.67	2.66	2.34	2.03

60-74 to 45-49	1.15	1.12	1.35	1.67	2.32	1.46	2.88	2.49	2.70	2.80
Percent of 60+ nonwhite	9.1%	7.1%	7.0%	7.8%	10.4%	12.5%	15.8%	19.6%	23.5%	26.6%
Sex Ratios:										
60-64	104.9	112.9	102.8	91.0	86.2	90.4	95.1	95.0	95.4	95.0
65-69	105.1	109.2	99.2	88.1	80.0	85.8	90.9	92.2	92.8	91.0
70-74	103.5	102.6	97.8	85.6	72.3	78.9	84.3	87.1	88.1	84.9
75-79	101.3	96.2	92.8	80.2	62.7	68.9	74.4	78.6	79.8	76.5
80-94	94.6	85.7	86.7	82.7	53.3	58.0	63.3	68.1	69.7	65.9
85+	79.4	76.4	75.2	63.8	43.7	40.1	42.7	48.8	50.1	44.2
60+	103.0	105.6	98.0	85.3	72.5	73.8	80.7	79.8	79.3	74.4

Source: See table 1.1

become increasingly nonwhite, largely paralleling projected changes in the total population (from 14 percent in 1980 to 27 percent in 2080). The reasons for the relative growth of the nonwhite population are threefold. First, the ultimate level of completed fertility (1.8 births per woman) is reached for nonblack races beginning with the birth cohort of 1985; for black women this level is not reached until calendar year 2050 (i.e., starting with birth cohorts of circa 2010). Second, by the year 2080, it is assumed that racial differences in mortality will have disappeared. Because of higher nonwhite mortality at present, the implication is that in the future mortality reductions among nonwhites will be greater than those for whites. More specifically, the middle level projections assume increases in life expectancy at birth of about 7 percent among whites, but of about 15 percent among blacks. Third, of the assumed annual population increase through net immigration of 500,000 persons, only 273,200 (or 55 percent) would be white. As noted above, currently some 86 percent of the United States' population is white.

The final panel of data in table 1.2 displays sex ratios by age within the older population. Because of historic patterns in immigration and mortality by gender, there has been a pronounced decline in the sex ratio at each age, with the extent of change increasing consistently with age. Overall, the sex ratio among the elderly has declined from 103 in 1900 to slightly more than 70 at present. This ratio is projected to remain comparatively stable throughout the projection period. At each age group, sex ratios are projected to increase by factors of about 10 percent, in part because of short-run decreases in male mortality relative to female mortality in the projection series. The age-specific increases in the sex ratio are largely offset by the aging of the older population, producing the observed stability in the sex ratio among the elderly.

DETERMINANTS OF
POPULATION AGING

As noted previously, both the absolute size of the older population and its share of the total population are dependent upon observed and projected levels of fertility, mortality, and international migration. At any given time, the number of new entrants into the older population will be a direct reflection of the number of births sixty years previously, as well as of the mortality experiences of that cohort. Additionally, net increments or decrements through international migration will have some, usually small, impact upon the number of the initial birth cohort who survive until age 60. Data that summarize the trends in the number of new entrants into the older population (shown as the size of the 60-69 age group at ten-year intervals from 1950 to 2080), the size of the 0-9 age group sixty years earlier, and the number of registered births in the United States sixty to sixty-nine years earlier are shown in table 2.1. Also shown in the table are what might be loosely termed "survival" rates; these are simply the ratios of the current size of the 60-69 age group either to the number of recorded births or to the enumerated size of the cohort when it was under ten years of age. Consistent with trends in mortality that may be observed during the twentieth century, these survival ratios have increased rather sharply over time. However, because relatively little further improvement in mortality is forecast at ages under 60, these ratios should increase only slightly in the future and not

Table 2.1
Components of Growth of the Population Aged 60-69,
United States, 1950-2080

Year	Persons (000s)	Births 60-69 years earlier	Persons aged 0-9 60 years earlier	"survival rates" from births	"survival rates" from census counts
1950	11,088	21,193	15,215	52.3%	72.9%
1960	13,400	23,923	18,079	56.0%	74.1%
1970	15,609	26,215	20,445	59.5%	76.3%
1980	18,870	28,557	23,051	66.1%	81.9%
1990	20,992	27,826	24,160	75.4%	86.9%
2000	20,190	24,162	21,324	83.6%	94.7%
2010	29,334	32,009	29,505	88.5%	96.0%
2020	37,743	40,686	39,013	92.8%	96.7%
2030	36,633	38,677	37,111	94.7%	98.7%
2040	32,572	33,279	33,048	97.9%	98.6%
2050	35,750	N.A.	36,786	N.A.	97.2%
2060	34,316	N.A.	35,024	N.A.	98.0%
2070	33,532	N.A.	33,839	N.A.	99.1%
2080	34,432	N.A.	34,637	N.A.	99.4%

Index to 1950

Year	Persons (000s)	Births 60-69 years earlier	Persons aged 0-9 60 years earlier
1950	100.0	100.0	100.0
1960	120.9	112.9	118.8
1970	140.8	123.7	134.4
1980	170.2	134.7	151.5
1990	189.3	131.3	158.8
2000	182.1	114.0	140.2
2010	255.5	151.0	193.9
2020	340.4	192.0	256.4
2030	330.4	182.5	243.9
2040	293.8	157.0	217.2
2050	322.4	N.A.	241.8
2060	309.5	N.A.	230.2
2070	302.4	N.A.	222.4
2080	310.5	N.A.	227.7

Source: See table 1.1

13

at all during the next century. Because the current size of each cohort includes the net effects of immigration, the so-called survival rates here are actually measuring the combined effects of mortality and international migration.

As can be seen from the second column, the size of the respective birth cohorts follows a generally upward trend through the year 2020, when the large birth cohorts of the 1950s attain the age of 60. Thereafter, there is a decline in the number of births through 2040 (the births of the 1970s). Although the size of the birth cohort of the 1980s has not yet been fully determined, an extrapolation of births recorded through 1988 suggests that the size of this birth cohort will be in the range of 36 to 38 million persons.

The lower panel of the table permits some assessment of the relative importance of the demographic processes in determining the number of new entrants into the older population at each point in time. The number of persons aged 60 to 69 at each ten-year interval represents the net number of new entrants; this is a function of births sixty to seventy years previous, as well as the decrements to that cohort through mortality and the net increment or decrement through international migration. The size of the net increment to the older population, relative to 1950, actually peaks in 2020, although it remains at about three times its 1950 level for all of the twenty-first century except in 2040, when the "baby bust" cohorts of the 1970s enter this population. In effect, the indices shown for the size of the birth cohort of sixty to seventy years previous and the size of the 0-9 age group enumerated sixty years previous suggest what the size of the group currently aged 60-69 would have been had not mortality (second column) or mortality and immigration (third column) changed as they in fact did. For example, in 2020, the size of the 60 to 69-year-old population will be some 37.7 million persons. Had the survival rate among the 40.7 million persons born between 1950 and 1960 been the same as that experienced by persons born between 1880 and 1890 (i.e., those aged 60 to 69 in 1950), there would have been only 21.3 million persons aged 60 to 69 in 2020 (discounting the cumulative effects of net immigration). Thus, of the 37.7 million 60-69-year-olds in 2020, some 56.8 percent is attributable to the increased size of the birth cohort (21 million in the 1880s versus 32 million in the 1940s), and the remainder is attributable to the combination of reductions in mortality, changes in net immigration, and changes in the quality of census enumeration of the 0-9 age group. For the remaining two years for which the size of the initial birth cohort is now known (2030 and 2040), this share diminishes to 55.6 and 54.7 percent, respectively. As a general statement, changes in the size of the initial birth cohort in the United States will be responsible for only slightly more than half of subsequent changes in the size of the 60 to 69 age group, and this proportion will diminish over time if assumptions about the future course of fertility prove to be accurate.

In general terms, the dynamics of the older population can be considered in a manner precisely analogous to that of the population as a whole. Persons are "born" into the population by attaining the minimum age (here 60) and exit by death or, rarely, by emigration. Consequently, the size, growth rate, and age structure of the older population will be determined by the interaction of these variables. The underlying projected dynamics of change within the older population of the United States from 1980 through 2080 are illustrated in table 2.2, which shows not only size and interperiod change but also the comparative contributions of "fertility" (aging in) and mortality among those included in the older population at the beginning of the period.

The impact of aging in can best be seen by considering the last line in each of the two panels; this shows the share of the older population at each time that is accounted for by those who have become "older" during the interval, that is, the share of the older population that is currently aged 60 to 69 years. After the dramatic increase during the first two decades of the coming century, when the baby boom generations account for more than half of the 60 + population, the net contribution of new entrants to the size of the older population remains quite stable at about 40 percent of the total. Similarly, the role of mortality (measured as the share of the beginning of period older population who survive until the end of period) is quite stable, with 60 to 65 percent surviving from one period to the next. Even though, as noted previously, the older population will be experiencing a substantial amount of aging during this period, the continual reductions in mortality throughout the projection period largely counterbalance the increase in the risk of death associated with the attainment of greater age. The reductions in the rate of increase within the older population, then, are the result of reductions in the rate at which new entrants come into the population and are not the result of increases in

Table 2.2
Projected Components of Change in the Population 60 Years Old
and Over, United States, 1980-2080

	1980 to 1990	1990 to 2000	2000 to 2010	2010 to 2020	2020 to 2030
Population:					
at start	35,637	42,301	45,581	55,533	72,343
at end	42,301	45,581	55,533	72,343	83,279
Increase:					
numeric	6,664	3,280	9,952	16,810	10,936
percent	18.7%	7.8%	21.8%	30.3%	15.1%
Survivors:					
numeric	21,309	25,391	27,199	34,600	46,646
percent	59.8%	60.0%	59.7%	62.3%	64.5%
Deaths to initial population	14,328	16,910	18,382	20,933	25,697
New entrants:					
numeric	20,992	20,190	28,334	37,743	36,633
percent of total	49.6%	44.3%	51.0%	52.2%	44.0%

16

	2030 to 2040	2040 to 2050	2050 to 2060	2060 to 2070	2070 to 2080
Population:					
at start	83,279	84,838	86,957	87,402	87,646
at end	84,838	86,957	87,402	87,646	89,112
Increase:					
numeric	1,559	2,119	445	244	1,466
percent	1.9%	2.5%	.5%	.3%	1.7%
Survivors:					
numeric	52,266	51,207	53,086	54,114	54,680
percent	62.8%	60.4%	61.0%	61.9%	62.4%
Deaths to initial population	31,013	33,631	33,871	33,288	32,966
New entrants:					
numeric	32,572	35,750	34,316	33,532	34,432
percent of total	39.4%	41.1%	39.3%	38.3%	39.6%

Source: See table 1.1

17

mortality among the existing population. Analogous to a situation
in any population characterized by declining fertility and stable or
decreasing mortality, the result here is the aging of the population. This result is illustrated in figure 2.1, which shows average
annual rates of increase among the population aged 60 and over
and average annual change in the mean age of this population (the
latter multiplied by 10 for reasons of scaling). The inverse relationship between these changes is quite apparent: periods of higher
growth among the elderly correspond quite naturally with relatively large numbers of new entrants into the older population.
These large numbers of persons aged 60 to 69 (end of period) serve
to lower the mean age within the older population.

It would prove difficult to overestimate the importance of mortality changes in accounting for previous and, in particular, future
evolutions in the size and demographic composition of the older
population of the United States. Mortality impacts upon the relative and absolute size of the older population in two important
ways. First, prevailing mortality at ages from birth to 59 determines the share of an initial birth cohort that will survive to attain
the age of 60. Second, mortality levels at age 60 and beyond deter-
mine the share of the older population that survives from period to
period; this fact, in conjunction with the number of new entrants
into the older population, determines the size and structure of the
older population at any time.

The data shown in table 2.3 present the proportions of birth cohorts surviving to age 60 for persons born between 1900 (the earliest year available) and 2020 (those reaching age 60 in 2080). The
data shown are of two types: the period-specific proportions,
which simply reflect the mortality rates prevailing at the time of
birth, and the cohort-specific proportions, which reflect the actual
or projected experiences of each cohort. Cohort rates are always
greater than the corresponding period rates because of actual and
projected declines in period mortality below that prevailing at the
time of the birth of the cohort. For both types of rate, there have
been considerable increases in the shares of birth cohorts actually
surviving or likely to survive to age 60. Among whites, there have
been increases on the order of 75 percent in the period rates for
current birth cohorts relative to persons born at the beginning of
the twentieth century; for future birth cohorts, survival prob-
abilities will increase only slightly, on the order of 5 to 8 percent.
The trends in the cohort rates are similar, with survival chances

Figure 2.1
Average Annual Change in Population Size and Mean Age,
Persons Aged 60 and Over, 1980-2080

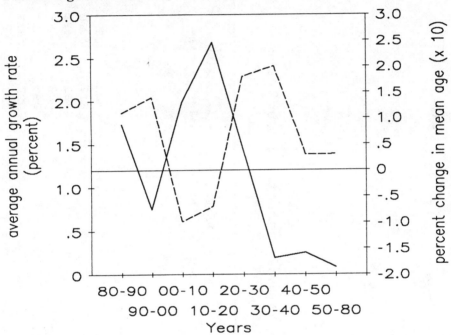

LEGEND

_____ Pop. Size

_ _ _ _. Mean Age

Source: Spencer, 1989, pp. 38-105.

Table 2.3
Proportions of Birth Cohorts Surviving to Age 60, by Race and
Gender, United States, 1900-2020

Period Rates	White Male	Nonwhite Male	White Female	Nonwhite Female
Year of Birth				
1900	.465	.242	.508	.275
1920	.585	.405	.617	.380
1940	.678	.444	.762	.491
1960	.755	.617	.863	.699
1980	.806	.691	.895	.820
2000	.869	.770	.927	.879
2020	.878	.808	.932	.900

Cohort Rates

Year of
Birth

1900	.550	.278	.630	.316
1920	.671	.502	.772	.572
1940	.786	.615	.865	.749
1960	.864	.742	.912	.851
1980	.874	.807	.929	.894
2000	.890	.835	.934	.912
2020	.884	.861	.936	.926

Sources: Decennial Censuses of Population
National Center for Health Statistics, 1988, p. 12
Spencer, 1984, p. 138-157

among already born cohorts increasing by some 50 to 60 percent from the beginning of the century to the present; increases among future cohorts are likely to be minimal, as relatively little gain in mortality among younger persons is embodied in the midrange mortality projections under discussion here.

For the nonwhite population, actual and prospective increases in survival proportions are somewhat greater: both period- and cohort-specific measures nearly tripled between the birth cohorts of 1900 and those of 1980. Increases in future survivorship are also likely to be greater among nonwhites than among whites, especially in terms of period measures, which are projected to rise by an additional 10 to 20 percent. This trend is the result of the assumption explicitly made in the projections that racial differences in mortality will cease to exist by the year 2080. Because of current differentials in favor of the white population, this assumption necessarily entails relatively greater mortality reduction within the nonwhite population.

Changes in mortality at ages 60 and above will affect the size and structure of the older population. A simple means of summarizing actual and prospective change in mortality at the older ages is the expectation of life at fixed ages. The data in table 2.4 show observed and forecast life expectancy, by race and gender, at age 65. Once again, the data are displayed in twenty-year increments, beginning in 1900. The data in table 2.4 show that thus far during the twentieth century, life expectancy at age 65 has increased by anywhere from 24 to 54 percent; increases have been greater among females than among males and greater among nonwhites than among whites. As a result of these differences, life expectancy at age 65 for white males, which was 94 percent of that of white females in 1900, stands now at only 77 percent; life expectancy of nonwhite males similarly declined from 85 to 74 percent of the level prevailing among white females. Conversely, nonwhite females improved their relative life expectancy at age 65, increasing from 93 to 95 percent of the white female level. For future years, essentially no change is likely for the position of white males relative to that of white females. However, for nonwhites, regardless of gender, improvements of about 6 percent relative to white females are projected.

Although not shown separately here, among persons aged 75 and over, a certain degree of irregularity may be observed in the historical data on life expectancy, especially among nonwhites.

One may observe, for example, sudden increases and decreases in life expectancy at age 75 for nonwhite males relative to nonwhite females and similarly irregular (though consistently higher) fluctuations among nonwhite females. Two separate phenomena are present here. First, the quality of census enumeration (and hence the denominators of the death rates that underlie the life table) for nonwhites has been rather questionable, especially in earlier years (Coale and Rives, 1973; Fay, Passel, and Robinson, 1988; Siegel, 1974). Consequently, if the quality of death registration data is superior to that of the enumeration and if, in fact, the enumerated data reflect the tendency to exaggerate age, then death rates are understated and life expectation is overstated. Second, despite these problems, there is evidence that the so-called mortality crossover effect between nonwhites and whites is a real occurrence (Manton and Stallard, 1984; Nam, Weatherby, and Ockay, 1978). Consequently, it is probably a fair assessment that the approximate equality of life expectation at age 75 that is currently observable within genders is accurate. This fact, coupled with the gradual cessation of race-specific mortality differences, yields the observed pattern of no future change in racial or gender differentials in life expectancy at age 75.

More detail on observed levels of mortality change among the elderly in the United States is presented in table 2.5, which shows changes in age-specific mortality by gender from 1940 through 1985. During this forty-five-year period, age-specific mortality among older males fell by a factor of about one-third, except for those aged 85 and over, for whom the decline was only about one-fourth (in large part because of the changed age structure of the population in this age category). Among older females, mortality levels in 1985 were almost uniformly about half their 1940 levels, again save the oldest old age group. To put these changes in some context, overall mortality in the United States declined by about 20 percent during this period (but by half when standardized to the 1940 age structure). Overall mortality among the elderly declined by about one-fourth, but when allowances are made for the changed age structure of the older population in the United States, the overall mortality reduction is on the order of 40 percent.

Among the older population as a whole, relative large mortality declines are concentrated in the decades of the 1940s and 1970s. During these periods, the age adjusted death rate among all persons aged 60 and over declined at an annual average rate of 1.7

Table 2.4
Life Expectancy at Age 65, by Race and Gender, 1900-2080

Year	White Male	Index to 1900	Other Male	Index to 1900	White Female	Index to 1900	Other Female	Index to 1900
1900	11.5		10.4		12.2		11.4	
1920	12.2	106.1	12.1	116.3	12.8	104.9	12.4	108.9
1940	12.1	105.2	12.2	117.3	13.6	111.5	14.0	122.8
1960	13.0	113.0	12.8	123.1	15.9	130.3	15.1	132.5
1980	14.3	124.3	13.8	132.7	18.6	152.5	17.6	154.4
2000	15.8	137.4	14.8	142.3	20.4	167.2	19.2	169.4
2020	16.7	145.2	15.9	152.9	21.5	176.2	20.6	180.7
2040	17.4	151.3	16.9	162.5	22.3	182.8	21.7	190.4
2060	18.1	157.4	17.9	172.1	23.1	189.3	22.8	200.0
2080	18.9	163.5	18.8	180.9	23.9	195.9	23.9	209.6

INDEX TO WHITE FEMALE

Year	White Male	Other Male	Other Female
1900	94.3%	85.2%	93.4%
1920	95.3%	94.5%	96.9%
1940	89.0%	89.7%	102.9%
1960	81.8%	80.5%	95.0%
1980	76.9%	74.2%	94.6%
2000	77.5%	72.5%	94.1%
2020	77.7%	74.0%	95.8%
2040	78.0%	75.8%	97.3%
2060	78.4%	77.5%	99.7%
2080	78.7%	78.7%	100.0%

Sources: US National Center for Health Statistics, 1989, p. 12
Spencer, 1989, p. 153

Note: Data for persons of other races are for blacks only
after 1980

Table 2.5
Age-specific Death Rates, Persons aged 60+, by Gender,
United States, 1940-1985 (rates per thousand)

Total	60-64	65-69	70-74	75-79	80-84	85+	Mean Age at Death
1940	26.7	39.7	61.1	94.8	145.6	235.7	73.9
1950	23.1	33.8	51.5	78.9	120.9	202.0	74.4
1960	21.5	31.4	47.2	72.0	117.2	198.6	75.3
1970	19.9	29.7	43.7	67.2	101.6	175.4	75.9
1980	16.5	24.6	36.8	55.0	86.4	159.8	76.8
1985	15.6	23.0	35.1	52.8	83.7	154.8	77.2

Male	60-64	65-69	70-74	75-79	80-84	85+	Mean Age at Death
1940	31.3	45.5	68.0	103.7	156.6	246.4	73.3
1950	28.9	41.6	60.6	89.6	133.4	216.4	73.5
1960	28.6	41.4	59.5	86.2	133.7	211.9	74.2
1970	27.7	41.2	58.9	86.8	123.9	197.7	74.5
1980	22.3	33.9	50.8	74.8	112.4	188.0	75.2
1985	20.6	30.6	47.5	71.4	110.2	183.3	75.5

Female	60-64	65-69	70-74	75-79	80-84	85+	Mean Age at Death
1940	21.9	33.9	54.3	86.5	136.0	227.6	74.7
1950	17.4	26.4	43.2	69.6	110.7	191.9	75.4
1960	15.0	22.6	36.7	60.7	105.3	190.1	76.6
1970	13.1	20.4	32.4	53.8	87.7	163.5	77.4
1980	11.4	17.2	26.7	42.6	72.6	147.5	78.4
1985	11.2	16.7	26.0	40.9	69.6	143.4	77.2

Percent Change:

Total	60-64	65-69	70-74	75-79	80-84	85+	Mean Age at Death
1950/1940	-13.5%	-14.9%	-15.7%	-16.8%	-17.0%	-14.3%	.7%
1960/1950	-6.9%	-7.1%	-8.3%	-8.7%	-3.1%	-1.7%	1.2%
1970/1960	-7.4%	-5.4%	-7.4%	-6.7%	-13.3%	-11.7%	.8%
1980/1970	-17.1%	-17.2%	-15.8%	-18.2%	-15.0%	-8.9%	1.2%
1985/1980	-5.5%	-6.5%	-4.6%	-4.0%	-3.1%	-3.1%	.5%
1985/1940	-41.6%	-42.1%	-42.6%	-44.3%	-42.5%	-34.3%	4.5%

Male	60-64	65-69	70-74	75-79	80-84	85+	Mean Age at Death
1950/1940	-7.7%	-8.6%	-10.9%	-13.6%	-14.8%	-12.2%	.3%
1960/1950	-1.0%	-.5%	-1.8%	-3.8%	.2%	-2.1%	1.0%
1970/1960	-3.1%	-.5%	-1.0%	.7%	-7.3%	-6.7%	.4%
1980/1970	-19.5%	-17.7%	-13.8%	-13.8%	-9.3%	-4.9%	.9%
1985/1980	-7.6%	-9.7%	-6.5%	-4.5%	-2.0%	-2.5%	.4%
1985/1940	-34.2%	-32.7%	-30.1%	-31.1%	-29.6%	-25.6%	3.0%

Table 2.5 (continued)

Female	60-64	65-69	70-74	75-79	80-84	85+	Mean Age at Death
1950/1940	-20.5%	-22.1%	-20.4%	-19.5%	-18.6%	-15.7%	.9%
1960/1950	-13.8%	-14.4%	-15.0%	-12.8%	-4.9%	-.9%	1.6%
1970/1960	-12.7%	-9.7%	-11.7%	-11.4%	-16.7%	-14.0%	1.0%
1980/1970	-13.0%	-15.7%	-17.6%	-20.8%	-17.2%	-9.8%	1.3%
1985/1980	-1.8%	-2.9%	-2.6%	-4.0%	-4.1%	-2.8%	-1.5%
1985/1940	-48.9%	-50.7%	-52.1%	-52.7%	-48.8%	-37.0%	3.3%

Male/Fem.	60-64	65-69	70-74	75-79	80-84	85+	Mean Age at Death
1940	142.9	134.2	125.2	119.9	115.1	108.3	98.1
1950	166.1	157.6	140.3	128.7	120.5	112.8	97.5
1960	190.7	183.2	162.1	142.0	127.0	111.5	96.9
1970	211.5	202.0	181.8	161.3	141.3	120.9	96.3
1980	195.6	197.1	190.3	175.6	154.8	127.5	95.5
1985	183.9	183.2	182.7	174.6	158.3	127.8	97.8

Sources: Fingerhut, 1984, p. 8-10
US National Center for Health Statistics, 1987a, p. 13

percent, more than twice the level of the 1950s, 1960s, and the first half of the 1980s. This pattern is generally true for each age group, although at ages 80 and over, relatively larger declines are to be observed in the 1960s as well. The mean age at death among persons aged 60 and over has risen rather steadily throughout the period from 74 years in 1940 to 77 years in 1985.

Temporal patterns of male mortality decline generally follow those for the entire population, although some important differences may be noted. Mortality declines among males in their 60s and early 70s were much greater during the 1970s than in previous decades, and, unlike overall mortality at these ages, this robust decline has continued into the present decade. Conversely, reductions in mortality at ages 80 and higher are much more concentrated in the decade of the 1940s and have been relatively small in recent years. Mortality declined at these ages to an equal or greater extent than at ages 60 to 79 until 1970; thereafter, mortality reduction among oldest old men has lagged behind that among younger men.

Mortality reductions among females are also concentrated in the 1940s and 1970s, although declines in the intervening decades were appreciably greater than those observed among males. Declines in female mortality at all ages and for all time periods were relatively and absolutely greater than those recorded for males until the present decade, with the exception of mortality change during the 1970s among persons aged 60 to 69. Thus, as shown in the bottom panel of table 2.5, the level of excess male mortality steadily increased at all ages through 1970. The trend in improvement in male mortality at the younger old ages has continued into the present decade and now includes all age groups from 60 to 79 years of age. At present, it is perhaps too early to state with any confidence whether this phenomenon represents a temporary perturbation in an established pattern of gender-specific mortality differences or represents the beginning of a closure in the gender differential that is due, perhaps, to greater female labor force activity.

Underlying the observed pattern of change in age-specific mortality is the pattern of changes in the cause structure of deaths within each age group. Because of revisions in the International Classification of Diseases (ICD) codes, it is possible to present consistent data on cause-specific mortality within the older population only for years subsequent to 1970. These are shown in table 2.6, which

Table 2.6
Deaths Rates by Principal Cause and Age, United States, 1970-1985
(rates per 100,00 persons)

Ages 65-74

	Cancer	Diabetes	Heart disease	Cerebro-vascular	Pneumonia	Arterio-scler.	Bron-chitis	Accidents	Other	Total
1970:										
rate	754	92	1558	384	90	37	87	86	494	3593
share	21.1%	2.6%	43.5%	10.7%	2.5%	1.0%	2.4%	2.4%	13.8%	
1975:										
rate	776	75	1323	303	70	27	65	67	483	3189
share	24.3%	2.4%	41.5%	9.5%	2.2%	.8%	2.0%	2.1%	15.1%	
1980:										
rate	818	65	1219	220	56	24	46	58	491	2995
share	27.3%	2.2%	40.7%	7.3%	1.9%	.8%	1.5%	1.9%	16.4%	
1985:										
rate	838	60	1081	171	58	17	43	51	520	2839
share	29.5%	2.1%	38.1%	6.0%	2.0%	.6%	1.5%	1.8%	18.3%	

Ages 75-84

Year											
1970: rate	1169	187	3684	1254	273	198	129	175	936	8004	
share	14.6%	2.3%	46.0%	15.7%	3.4%	2.5%	1.6%	2.2%	11.7%		
1975: rate	1222	160	3281	1076	264	159	106	141	949	7359	
share	16.6%	2.2%	44.6%	14.6%	3.6%	2.2%	1.4%	1.9%	12.9%		
1980: rate	1232	131	2993	789	220	126	78	120	1004	6690	
share	18.4%	2.0%	44.7%	11.8%	3.3%	1.9%	1.2%	1.8%	15.0%		
1985: rate	1281	128	2713	606	241	82	75	108	1211	6445	
share	19.9%	2.0%	42.1%	9.4%	3.7%	1.3%	1.2%	1.7%	18.8%		

Ages 85+

Year											
1970: rate	1321	230	7891	3014	815	880	121	393	1680	16344	
share	8.1%	1.4%	48.3%	18.4%	5.0%	5.4%	.7%	2.4%	10.3%		
1975: rate	1409	225	7282	2655	777	707	101	317	1716	15187	
share	9.3%	1.5%	47.9%	17.5%	5.1%	4.7%	.7%	2.1%	11.3%		
1980: rate	1595	222	7777	2289	886	657	92	293	2172	15980	
share	10.0%	1.4%	48.7%	14.3%	5.5%	4.1%	.6%	1.8%	13.6%		
1985: rate	1592	215	7275	1838	1024	466	90	254	2728	15480	
share	10.3%	1.4%	47.0%	11.9%	6.6%	3.0%	.6%	1.6%	17.6%		

Table 2.6 (continued)

	Cancer	Diabetes	Heart disease	Cerebro- vascular	Pneumonia	Arterio- scler.	Bron- chitis	Accidents	Other	Total
Percent change: 65-74										
1970-75	2.8%	-18.3%	-15.0%	-21.1%	-22.2%	-28.7%	-24.6%	-22.3%	-2.3%	-11%
1975-80	5.5%	-13.7%	-7.9%	-27.6%	-20.8%	-11.3%	-29.6%	-13.2%	1.7%	-6%
1980-85	2.5%	-8.0%	-11.3%	-22.0%	4.0%	-28.0%	-6.5%	-12.5%	6.0%	-5%
1970-85	11.2%	-35.2%	-30.7%	-55.4%	-35.9%	-54.4%	-50.3%	-41.0%	5.3%	-21%
share	40.3%	-18.2%	-12.5%	-43.7%	-19.1%	-42.5%	-37.3%	-25.5%	32.9%	
Percent change: 75-84										
1970-75	4.5%	-14.3%	-10.9%	-14.2%	-3.1%	-19.4%	-17.7%	-19.3%	1.4%	-8%
1975-80	0.9%	-18.1%	-8.8%	-26.7%	-16.8%	-21.3%	-26.9%	-14.7%	5.8%	-9%
1980-85	4.0%	-2.3%	-9.4%	-23.2%	9.7%	-34.4%	-3.0%	-10.5%	20.6%	-4%
1970-85	9.6%	-31.4%	-26.4%	-51.7%	-11.5%	-58.4%	-41.7%	-39.4%	29.4%	-19%
share	36.1%	-14.8%	-8.5%	-40.0%	9.9%	-48.3%	-27.6%	-23.4%	60.7%	
Percent change: 85+										
1970-75	6.7%	-2.4%	-7.7%	-11.3%	-4.6%	-19.7%	-16.4%	-19.3%	2.1%	-7%
1975-80	13.2%	-1.2%	6.8%	-13.8%	14.0%	-7.1%	-9.6%	-7.7%	26.6%	5%
1980-85	-0.2%	-3.2%	-6.5%	-19.7%	15.6%	-29.0%	-2.3%	-13.1%	25.6%	-3%
1970-85	20.5%	-6.6%	-7.8%	-39.0%	25.7%	-47.1%	-26.2%	-35.2%	62.4%	-5%
share	27.2%	-1.4%	-2.7%	-35.6%	32.7%	-44.1%	-22.0%	-31.6%	71.5%	

Sources: see table 2.5

shows age-specific mortality for the eight most frequent causes of death among the elderly, for 1970, 1975, 1980, and 1985. Data are shown for the three broad age groups 65-74, 75-84, and 85+.

Mortality rates for each cause and for all causes increase with age. In general, overall mortality levels among persons aged 65-74 were about 45 percent of levels at ages 75-84, which, in turn, were about 48 percent of observed levels at ages 85 and over in 1970 and 1975 and about 41 percent of these levels in 1980 and 1985. Of the three principal causes of death, heart disease closely follows the overall pattern, as age-specific rates more than double from ages 65-74 to ages 75-84 and again from 75-84 to 85 and over. Cancer mortality increases somewhat less with age (about 50 percent from 65-74 to 75-84 and then by about 20 percent), while the incidence of cerebrovascular disease mortality increases sharply with age, rising by a factor of nearly 2.5 between ages 65-74 and 75-84 and by a factor of more than 1.6 between the latter age and 85+.

During the fifteen-year period in question, total mortality among persons aged 65-74 and 75-84 dropped by about 20 percent, while a smaller decline of about 5 percent could be seen among those aged 85 and over (again, the latter result will partially reflect the aging of the oldest old population). Changes in the structure of causes of death are quite consistent among persons aged 65 to 84. Both age groups experienced declines of 30 to 40 percent in the rate of death attributed to heart disease, diabetes, and accidents and declines of about 50 percent in mortality rates due to cerebrovascular conditions, arteriosclerosis, and bronchitis. However, cancer mortality rates in each of these groups rose by about 10 percent during this period. Heart disease and cancer have been jointly responsible for about two-thirds of all deaths occurring at these ages throughout the period. With the substantial reduction in mortality due to heart disease and the rise in cancer mortality, the relative importance of these factors shifted over the period. The share of deaths due to cancer rose from 21 to 30 percent among those aged 65 to 74 and from 15 to 20 percent among those aged 75 to 84. Conversely, the share of deaths attributable to heart disease declined from 44 to 38 percent and from 46 to 42 percent, respectively. The relative importance of all other causes of death, other than the residual category, declined in each age group except for a slight rise in the share of deaths due to pneumonia among persons aged 75 to 84.

Reductions in death rates among the oldest old were of similar orders of magnitude as those for the younger elderly for deaths due to accidents and arteriorsclerosis and were substantial, though lower, for bronchitis and cerebrovascular disease. Declines in heart disease- and diabetes-related mortality were much below those occurring among persons aged 65 to 84, while the increase in cancer and all-other mortality was at least twice that among the younger elderly. Although cancer is much less important as a cause of death among the oldest old, the share of deaths due to cancer in this segment of the population rose from 8 to 10 percent during the fifteen-year interval. The proportion of deaths due to cerebrovascular disease, the second cause of death at this age, declined from 18 to 12 percent, while heart disease accounted for a constant 47-48 percent of deaths throughout the period.

Differences in the comparative importance of the various causes of death exist with respect to demographic parameters other than age. The data in table 2.7 provide summaries of current differences between genders and racial groups, within the same three broad age groups utilized in table 2.6. The data shown here are simple averages of single-year data for 1972, 1978, and 1982. These years are chosen because they are approximately midway through each of the five-year periods for which data were presented in table 2.6 and collectively may be viewed as representing the pattern of gender- and race-specific differentials that existed with respect to the distribution of deaths by principal cause.

Male mortality exceeds female mortality for all causes and for each of the three principal causes, with the trivial exception of approximate equality in cerebrovascular disease mortality levels in the oldest ages. However, the relative differential for both the latter cause and heart disease diminishes consistently with age (as does overall mortality), while the differential for cancer mortality remains constant at a level of nearly 2 to 1. Because of this constancy, cancer is relatively more important as a cause of death among men aged 75 and over than among women within this age range. Conversely, heart disease mortality, which is more important among men at ages 65 to 74 (relative to women), becomes relatively less important after age 75. The share of deaths attributable to stroke and associated conditions is consistently about three-fourths as large among men as among women.

In somewhat the same manner as the gender differential in mortality, the racial differential also diminishes with increasing age, but to a much greater extent. Nonwhite mortality from all causes exceeds the level among whites by about a fourth at ages 65 to 74, is approximately equal at ages 75 to 84, and is nearly one-third lower at ages 85 and older. Each of the three principal causes follows this general pattern, although the decline in the cancer mortality differential is relatively modest and that for stroke mortality is quite pronounced. Changes in the relative portions of deaths attributable to each cause follow logically from these observations; the share of deaths due to cancer rises from slightly below to slightly above the corresponding share in the white population, the relative share due to heart disease remains at about 90 percent across the older age spectrum, and the relative share attributable to cerebrovascular disease and arteriosclerosis declines markedly.

Thus far, our considerations regarding the future course of aging in the United States have been predicated upon the so-called middle variant in mortality. It may be recalled that this level of mortality assumes increases in longevity from 25 to 35 percent at age 60 and from 40 to 50 percent at age 75. The 1984 set of U.S. Bureau of the Census population projections is the first that incorporated alternative assumptions about the future course of mortality. The reasons for the development of alternative mortality series may be summarized as follows:

The major reason for this change is that, with the stability of fertility rates in recent years, mortality forecast errors have become a significant proportion of the overall error. Mortality accounted for more than 40 percent of the 6-year aggregate error in the last two projections. Another reason is that *all Census Bureau projections made in the last 25 years have been too conservative with respect to declines in mortality.* Those made since the late 1960's, in fact, have projected at least 8 percent too many deaths by the 6th year of their projection period. (Spencer, 1984, p. 17, emphasis added)

To illustrate this point slightly further, the most recent projections prior to the 1980 census, which were released in 1977 (U.S. Bureau of the Census, 1977), underprojected the total size of the U.S. population by 5.6 million persons (or 2.5 percent) in the year 1980. Although causes other than mortality may be identified for such a large error in such a short period of time (most notably, the probable inclusion of undocumented aliens in the census enumeration), the population aged 60 and over was underprojected by 1.1

Table 2.7
Gender and Race Differentials in Mortality, by Cause, United States, 1972, 1978, and 1982 (rates per 100,000, average of three years)

(rates per 100,000, average of three years)

	65 to 74		75 to 84		85 and over	
	rate	share	rate	share	rate	share
All Deaths	3,034		6,959		14,979	
Male	4,176		9,099		17,538	
Female	2,156		5,671		13,489	
White	2,964		6,956		15,440	
Other	3,683		6,993		10,497	
Cancer	800	26.4%	1,251	18.0%	1,486	9.9%
Male	1,074	25.7%	1,792	19.7%	2,178	12.4%
Female	590	27.4%	927	16.3%	1,175	9.7%
White	790	26.7%	1,249	18.0%	1,518	9.8%
Other	894	24.3%	1,280	18.3%	1,185	11.3%
Heart Disease	1,237	40.8%	3,091	44.4%	7,236	48.3%
Male	1,763	42.2%	3,944	43.3%	8,129	46.3%
Female	833	38.6%	2,578	45.5%	6,832	50.6%
White	1,222	41.2%	3,116	44.8%	7,501	48.6%
Other	1,378	37.4%	2,819	40.3%	4,649	44.3%

36

Cerebrovascular and Arteriosclerosis						
Male	271	8.9%	1,023	14.7%	2,948	19.7%
Female	324	7.8%	1,121	12.3%	2,916	16.6%
Female	229	10.6%	964	17.0%	2,962	22.0%
White	251	8.5%	1,015	14.6%	3,054	19.8%
Other	450	12.2%	1,115	16.0%	1,923	18.3%

Male to Female Ratio:

All Deaths	1.94		1.60		1.30	
Cancer	1.92	.94	1.93	1.21	1.85	1.43
Heart Disease	2.11	1.09	1.53	.95	1.19	.92
Cerebrovascular & Arteriosclerosis	1.41	.73	1.16	.72	.98	.76

Nonwhite to White ratio:

All Deaths	1.24		1.01		.69	
Cancer	1.13	.91	1.02	1.02	.78	1.15
Heart Disease	1.13	.91	.90	.90	.62	.91
Cerebrovascular & Arteriosclerosis	1.79	1.44	1.10	1.09	.63	.93

Sources: Fingerhut, 1984, p. 12-21

million persons or some 3.3 percent of its estimated (based upon census results) size in mid-1980 (U.S. Bureau of the Census, 1988d).

Table 2.8 presents the levels of life expectancy at birth as well as at age 65 for the low and middle level mortality assumptions for the beginning of each decade in the projection period as well as at ages 75 and 85 for those times that are available. Although a high mortality variant also exists (with terminal life expectancies at birth of 74.7 for men and 81.3 for women), there seems at present little likelihood that the minimal improvements in mortality that are embodied in these assumptions will reflect reality. As can be seen from the bottom line of table 2.8, the overall differences in the extension of life expectancy are six years for men and seven years for women. Male life expectancy under the midrange assumption increases by 9 percent, from seventy-two to seventy-eight years; under the low mortality regime the increase is 19 percent, to eighty-five years. Life expectancy increases among women are slightly greater, being seven or thirteen years (8 and 16 percent) for the middle and low assumptions, respectively.

The data shown in the columns to the right indicate that relative mortality increases are a positive function of age. Not only is the percentage increase in life expectancy greater with advancing age, but the relative difference between the low and middle variants also widens with age. While the difference in the increase in life expectancy at birth between the low and medium mortality variants is 113 percent for males and 108 percent for females, this difference expands to 141 and 114 percent at age 65, to 152 and 115 percent at age 75, and to 157 and 128 percent at age 85.

This finding suggests that a disproportionate and increasing share of the additional years of life added by the adoption of the low rather than the medium level mortality assumption is to be found in the years at the end of the age span. This suggestion is illustrated by figure 2.2, which shows the proportions of total years of "additional" life represented by the low variant that will occur at ages 60 and 90. Even as early in the projection period as 1990, more than half of additional male years of life and three-fourths of additional female years occur at ages 67 and above, and 30 to 39 percent occurs at ages 90 and above. By the end of the projection period, these proportions rise to 80 and 90 percent at age 60 and to 63 and 74 percent at age 90.

Table 2.8
Differences in Life Expectancy at Selected Ages, Low and Medium Mortality Assumptions, United States, 1986-2080

	at birth		at age 65		at age 75		at age 85	
	male	female	male	female	male	female	male	female
1986	71.5	78.5	14.8	19.0	9.4	12.2	5.8	7.2
1990: mid	72.1	79.0	15.0	19.4				
low	72.7	79.5	15.4	19.6				
2000: mid	73.5	80.4	15.7	20.3				
low	75.6	82.1	16.9	21.3				
2005: mid	74.2	81.0	16.0	20.8	10.3	13.8	6.3	8.2
low	77.1	83.4	17.6	22.1	11.4	14.8	7.0	9.1
2010: mid	74.4	81.3	16.2	21.0				
low	77.6	83.9	18.1	22.6				
2020: mid	74.9	81.8	16.6	21.4				
low	78.7	85.0	19.0	23.6				
2030: mid	75.4	82.3	17.0	21.9				
low	79.7	86.0	19.9	24.6				

Table 2.8 (continued)

	at birth		at age 65		at age 75		at age 85	
	male	female	male	female	male	female	male	female
2040: mid	75.9	82.8	17.3	22.3				
low	80.8	87.1	20.9	25.6				
2050: mid	76.4	83.3	17.7	22.7				
low	81.8	88.2	21.8	26.6				
2060: mid	76.8	83.8	18.1	23.1				
low	82.9	89.3	22.7	27.6				
2070: mid	77.3	84.3	18.5	23.5				
low	83.9	90.3	23.6	28.6				
2080: mid	77.9	84.7	18.9	23.9	12.6	16.6	8.5	10.6
low	84.9	91.3	24.5	29.5	17.6	21.7	12.7	14.9
Percent Change:								
1986 to 2080:								
mid	6.8%	7.9%	27.4%	25.9%	34.8%	35.7%	47.0%	47.4%
low	19.7%	16.4%	66.0%	55.4%	97.7%	76.9%	121.0%	107.9%

Sources: see table 2.4

Figure 2.2
**Proportion of Additional Life Expectancy Occurring at Ages 65 +,
by Gender, 2000-2080**

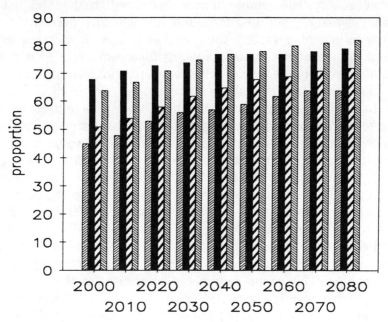

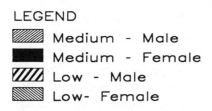

LEGEND
Medium - Male
Medium - Female
Low - Male
Low- Female

Source: Spencer, 1989, pp. 109-11.

41

As might be expected, sustained differences in the level of mortality such as those outlined here would have profound implications for the size and, especially, for the age composition of the older population of the United States. These changes are summarized in table 2.9, with the full details being displayed in appendix 3. These data show the number of persons who would be added to the total population and to age groups beginning with age 60 if the low, rather than the middle, range mortality assumptions were to reflect reality. The number of persons "added" to the total population increases from 171 thousand in 1990 (0.1 percent of the medium mortality variant total) to 25.4 million in 2080 (an increment to the medium variant of nearly 9 percent). A large majority of the incremental population is always to be found among persons aged 60 and above; the share at these ages rises from 68 percent at the beginning of the projection period to 87 percent at the end. However, an increasingly larger share of the increment is found among the oldest old. In 1990, lower mortality would imply the survival to ages 85 and above of an additional 26 thousand persons; these would account for about one-sixth of the increment to total population. Both the size of the increment to the oldest old and the proportion that this would represent of the total increment rise throughout the projection period. By the end of the period, in 2080, there would be more than 13 million additional persons aged 85 and over, if lower levels of mortality prevail throughout. This group represents 54 percent of the total increment in that year; it also represents an 81 percent increase over the size of the 85 and over population that would occur if medium, rather than low, mortality had prevailed.

The relative and absolute size of the increment to the older population as a result of lower mortality increases steadily through the projection period. Initially these increases are rather modest but would still result in the addition of more than 1 million persons (nearly 3 percent) as early as the turn of the century. By the year 2080, the size of the older population would have expanded by more than 22 million older persons (25 percent of the medium mortality baseline). Because this incremental population will be concentrated at the extreme upper end of the age distribution, there will be some impact upon the age structure of the older population. Under the assumptions of the medium level mortality projection, the mean age of the older population would rise from 71 years in 1980 to more than 75 years in 2080; with lower mortality, this mean age will rise by an additional two and one-half years. In order to give some flavor of the implications of low mortality for the older age structure, figure 2.3 shows the percentage of the population aged 60 and over in 2080 that would fall into each five-year age group. It is quite apparent that with lower mortality there are relatively more persons within each group, beginning at age 85.

The only component of change within the older population that has hitherto been ignored is international migration. From a historical perspective, migration to the United States has been a critical element of demographic development (Taeuber and Taeuber, 1971). The impact of international migration on population aging is only very slightly related to the immigration of older persons but rather is the result of immigrants at younger ages who remain in the United States and "age into" the ranks of the elderly along with the native-born population. Table 2.10 shows the share of the older population, by age, that was reported to have been born outside the United States at each census year from 1940 through 1980. The data shown pertain only to the white population until 1970. While about one-fourth of older whites in both 1940 and 1950 were foreign-born, this proportion declines quite markedly between 1960 and the present. The share of foreign-born is much lower among the younger white elderly of the present and is not likely to increase to any appreciable extent in the future. This situation, of course, reflects the observable dramatic changes in place of origin among recent immigrants to the United States and the probability that future cohorts of immigrants will be drawn from Asia and Latin America.

Although table 2.10 shows data on the share of foreign-born among older nonwhites in 1970 and 1980, the approximate doubling of these proportions cannot be taken at face value. There is a tendency for persons of Spanish origin to respond with an ethnic identifier (such as "Mexican," "Cuban," "Puerto Rican," and so on) to the census question on race. Prior to the 1980 census, responses of this type were coded as white; in 1980, these responses were coded as "other" (that is, races other than white, black, Asian, or native American). Because a relatively large share of persons falling into this category would have been born outside the United States, the reported increase in the foreign-born among the older nonwhite population must be viewed at least in part as being artifactual.

The impact of future levels of immigration to the United States

Table 2.9
Increments to Projected Population, Low versus Middle Mortality
Assumptions, United States, 1990-2080

	Thousands of persons	Percent of Total	Percent of Middle Mortality Projection
1990			
Total	171		.1%
60-69	35	20.5%	.2%
70-79	40	23.4%	.3%
80-94	15	8.3%	.4%
85+	26	15.2%	.8%
60+	116	67.8%	.3%
2000			
Total	1,836		.7%
60-69	319	17.4%	1.6%
70-79	432	23.5%	2.7%
80-94	184	10.0%	3.9%
85+	334	18.2%	7.2%
60+	1,269	69.1%	2.8%
2025			
Total	9,557		3.2%
60-69	1,831	19.2%	4.7%
70-79	2,525	26.4%	9.4%
90-94	1,049	11.0%	15.8%
85+	2,379	24.9%	33.9%
60+	7,784	81.4%	9.8%

44

2050

Total	18,212		6.1%
60-69	1,943	10.7%	5.4%
70-79	3,216	17.7%	12.2%
80-84	2,137	11.7%	22.2%
85+	8,373	46.0%	54.8%
60+	15,669	86.0%	18.0%

2080

Total	25,420		9.7%
60-69	2,087	8.2%	6.1%
70-79	3,851	15.1%	13.9%
80-84	2,608	10.3%	26.3%
85+	13,672	53.8%	80.6%
60+	22,218	87.4%	24.9%

Source: Computed from Spencer, 1989, p. 107 and 110

Figure 2.3
Age Composition of the Older Population in 2080, under Alternative Mortality Assumptions

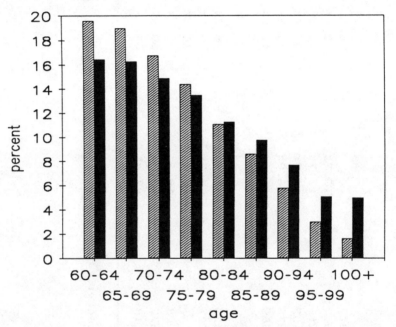

Source: Spencer, 1989, pp. 107, 110.

Table 2.10
Foreign-born Population Aged 60+, by Age and Race, United
States, 1940-1980

(percent of total)

White:	1940	1950	1960	1970	1980
60+	24.4%	23.6%	19.4%	14.2%	9.8%
60-64	24.2%	23.5%	16.3%	9.6%	5.2%
65-69	23.2%	24.3%	19.3%	13.6%	7.5%
70-74	25.1%	23.5%	22.2%	16.0%	10.4%
75+	26.0%	23.3%	21.4%	18.7%	16.2%
75-79			21.9%	20.1%	14.5%
80-84			21.0%	18.6%	16.7%
85+			20.2%	14.2%	19.1%
Nonwhite:					
60+				5.4%	11.7%
60-64				4.8%	10.8%
65-69				5.3%	10.9%
70-74				6.2%	11.9%
75+				5.9%	13.4%
75-79				6.1%	12.8%
80-84				6.2%	13.4%
85+				5.0%	15.3%

Source: Decennial Censuses of Population

47

upon the size and structure of the older population may be determined by considering population projections with alternative levels of migration. Current projections include three immigration alternatives whose age structure is summarized in appendix 4. As would be expected, the annual number of immigrants who would be at least 60 years of age is quite low and accounts for only a small fraction of total immigration. It is perhaps worthy of note that the high variant projects net outmigration at ages 75 and above and that the low and medium variants project net outmigration (in sum) among persons aged 60 and over.

The increments or decrements to the size of the older population for the high and low variants, relative to the medium (it is this latter series that has been incorporated in all projections discussed thus far), are summarized in table 2.11. The projections that are compared in this table also incorporate the medium variant assumptions with regard to both fertility and mortality. Although net migration differences make an appreciable difference to the size of the total population, the impact on the size of the older population is somewhat less. In the year 2025, for example, sustained high immigration (800 thousand persons per year) would add 14.9 million (5 percent) more persons to the total population than would middle immigration (500 thousand persons per year); the increment to the older population would be 1.1 million, or a 1 percent increase. Conversely, sustained low immigration (300 thousand persons per year) would lower the size of the total population by about 11 million persons (3.7 percent) and would lower the size of the population aged 60 and above by 1.4 million persons, or by 2 percent. Although the absolute and relative increments or decrements increase over time, it remains the case that the size of the older population is relatively less sensitive to immigration differentials than is the size of the younger population.

The impact of alternative levels of immigration upon the size of the older population relative to the whole or upon the age structure of the older population itself is comparatively trivial. At the end of the projection period, the share of population that is at least age 60 ranges from 29.6 (high immigration) to 31.0 (low) percent, as opposed to 30.5 percent for the middle level. Similarly, for the share of population aged 85 +, the range in 2080 is 5.5 to 6 percent (figures 2.4a, b).

Table 2.11
Increments to Projected Population, Low and High versus Middle
Net Immigration Assumptions, United States, 1990-2080

	High Net Immigration			Low Net Immigration		
	Persons (000s)	% of total	% of mid immigrtn.	Persons (000s)	% of total	% of mid immigrtn.
1990						
Total	962		.34%	-1211		-2.40%
60-69	19	2.20%	.09%	-34	2.81%	-.16%
70-79	3	.35%	.02%	-17	1.40%	-.12%
80-84	-1	-.12%	-.03%	-3	.25%	-.08%
85+	-6	-.70%	-.18%	-2	.17%	-.06%
60+	15	1.74%	.04%	-56	4.62%	-.13%
2000						
Total	4070		1.52%	-3978		-5.93%
60-69	86	2.11%	.43%	-125	3.14%	-.62%
70-79	40	.98%	.25%	-68	1.71%	-.42%
80-84	4	.10%	.08%	-14	.35%	-.30%
85+	-12	-.29%	-.26%	-9	.23%	-.19%
60+	118	2.90%	.26%	-216	5.43%	-.47%

Table 2.11 (continued)

	High Net Immigration			Low Net Immigration		
	Persons (000s)	% of total immigrtn.	% of mid immigrtn.	Persons (000s)	% of total immigrtn.	% of mid immigrtn.
2025						
Total	14917		5.00%	-11163		-3.74%
60-69	750	5.03%	1.91%	-864	7.74%	-2.21%
70-79	261	1.75%	.97%	-336	3.01%	-1.25%
90-94	55	.37%	.93%	-79	.71%	-1.19%
85+	31	.21%	.44%	-73	.65%	-1.04%
60+	1097	7.35%	1.38%	-1352	12.11%	-1.70%
2050						
Total	27164		9.06%	-18221		-6.08%
60-69	2444	9.00%	6.84%	-1792	9.83%	-5.01%
70-79	1589	5.85%	6.04%	-1295	7.11%	-4.92%
80-84	413	1.52%	4.30%	-422	2.32%	-4.39%
85+	294	1.08%	1.92%	-372	2.04%	-2.43%
60+	4740	17.45%	5.45%	-3881	21.30%	-4.46%
2080						
Total	40624		13.90%	-26377		-9.03%
60-69	4108	10.11%	11.93%	-2792	10.58%	-9.11%
70-79	3016	7.42%	10.85%	-2126	8.06%	-7.65%
80-84	966	2.38%	9.74%	-715	2.71%	-7.21%
85+	1283	3.16%	7.56%	-1000	3.79%	-5.99%
60+	9373	23.07%	10.52%	-6633	25.15%	-7.44%

Source: Computed from Spencer, 1989, p. 109-111

50

Figure 2.4a
Share of Population Aged 60+ under Alternative Immigration
Assumptions, 1990-2080

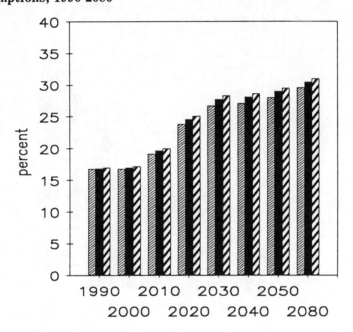

LEGEND
High Net Immigration
Middle Net Immigration
Low Net Immigration

Source: Spencer, 1989, pp. 109-11.

Figure 2.4b
Share of Population Aged 85+ under Alternative Immigration Assumptions, 1990-2080

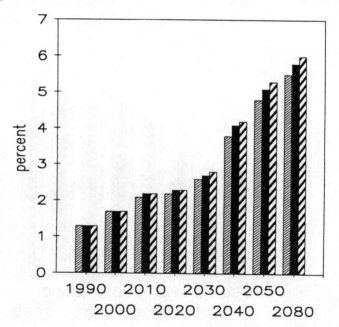

LEGEND

High Net Immigration
Medium Net Immigration
Low Net Immigration

Source: Spencer, 1989, pp. 109-11.

3

Population Distribution
and Migration

Analysis of the spatial distribution of any population can proceed along the lines of the size or functional characteristics of places of residence or, alternatively, along the geographical or regional composition of the population. In the first portion of this chapter, we will briefly describe the distribution of the older population of the United States in terms of its urban or rural residence; within the context of the urban population we consider the extent to which this population resides in so-called urban areas and metropolitan areas and, finally, consider the extent to which this population lives in the city proper or in the suburban areas that surround central cities.

Table 3.1 presents data on persons aged 60 and over, according to urban or rural residence in each census year from 1950 to 1980. The current definition of the urban population, which was adopted at the time of the 1950 census, includes all persons living in incorporated places of 2,500 or more inhabitants; census designated (nonincorporated) places; and other territory, regardless of municipal status, that is included in urbanized areas. The concept of an urbanized area is rather complex but essentially includes an incorporated place and adjacent densely settled surrounding area that together have a minimum population of 50,000. (U.S. Bureau of the Census, 1982). All population that is not urban is classified as rural.

Table 3.1
Persons Aged 60+ by Age, Urban-Rural and Metropolitan-
Nonmetropolitan Residence, United States, 1950-1980

Age	Total	Urban	Rural	Metro-politan	Nonmetro-politan	percent:	
						urban	metro
	(thousands of persons)						
1980:							
Total	226,546	167,051	59,495	169,431	57,115	73.7%	74.8%
60-64	10,088	7,423	2,664	7,375	2,712	73.6%	73.1%
65-69	8,782	6,424	2,359	6,260	2,523	73.1%	71.3%
70-74	6,798	5,032	1,766	4,805	1,993	74.0%	70.7%
75-79	4,794	3,614	1,180	3,397	1,397	75.4%	70.9%
80-84	2,935	2,249	686	2,088	847	76.6%	71.1%
85+	2,240	1,727	513	1,575	665	77.1%	70.3%
[60+]	35,637	26,469	9,168	25,500	10,137	74.3%	71.6%
[0-59]	190,909	140,582	50,327	143,930	46,978	73.6%	75.4%
1970:							
Total	203,212	149,325	53,887	153,624	49,589	73.5%	75.6%
60-64	8,617	6,239	2,378	6,269	2,347	72.4%	72.8%
65-69	6,992	5,054	1,937	5,018	1,973	72.3%	71.8%
70-74	5,444	3,981	1,462	3,901	1,543	73.1%	71.7%
75-79	3,835	2,813	1,022	2,716	1,119	73.4%	70.8%
90-84	2,284	1,676	608	1,597	687	73.4%	69.9%

85+	1,511	1,106	405	1,044	466	73.2%	69.1%
[60+]	28,682	20,870	7,813	20,546	8,137	72.3%	71.6%
[0-59]	174,530	128,455	46,074	133,078	41,451	73.6%	76.2%
1960:							
Total	179,323	125,269	54,054	112,984	66,439	69.9%	62.9%
60-64	7,142	5,091	2,052	4,483	2,659	71.3%	62.8%
65-69	6,258	4,402	1,856	3,789	2,469	70.3%	60.5%
70-74	4,739	3,314	1,425	2,790	1,949	69.9%	58.9%
75-79	3,054	2,101	953			68.8%	
80-84	1,590	1,078	502	3,066	2,497	68.2%	55.1%
85+	929	631	298			67.9%	
[60+]	23,702	16,617	7,085	14,128	9,575	70.1%	59.6%
[0-59]	155,621	108,652	46,969	98,756	56,965	69.8%	63.5%
1950:							
Total	151,326	96,847	54,479			64.0%	
60-64	6,074	4,039	2,036			66.5%	
65-69	5,014	3,243	1,770			64.7%	
70-74	3,419	2,178	1,241			63.7%	
75-79	3,284	2,060	1,224			62.7%	
80+	578	360	218			62.3%	
[60+]	18,369	11,880	6,490			64.7%	
[0-59]	132,957	84,967	47,989			63.9%	

Source: Decennial Censuses of Population

55

According to this definition, the total population of the United States has increased in terms of proportion classified as urban from about two-thirds in 1950 and 1960 to about three-fourths in both 1970 and 1980. The older population has followed the overall pattern extremely closely; the share of population urban among those aged 60 + has varied by less than one percentage point from that of the total population. Within age groups, the younger segments of the older population have tended to be marginally more urbanized at the time of the two earlier censuses but marginally less urbanized at the time of the two later censuses.

In addition to data on the urban population, table 3.1 also presents data on the metropolitan population from 1960 to 1980. The concept of metropolitan is generally similar to urban, except that metropolitan areas are defined on the basis of entire county units. In general, the majority of the population of a metropolitan area would be classified as urban, although most of these areas will also have some rural population as well. Not all urban population is necessarily metropolitan, especially for persons who live in small and comparatively isolated places. In any event, the share of both the younger and the older population that resides in metropolitan areas has been almost identical to that categorized as being urban since 1970. The elderly are perhaps slightly less likely than younger persons to be metropolitan; in contrast to the relationship between age (within the elderly) and urbanization, there is a general tendency for the younger elderly to be more likely to be metropolitan than are the older elderly.

One aspect of the older urban population that is worthy of some brief additional comment is the distribution of that population according to type of urban place of residence. For our purposes, the urban population can be divided into three distinct and exhaustive components: residents of central cities of urbanized areas, other residents of urbanized areas (that is, residents of suburban areas), and residents of urban places outside urbanized areas (that is, residents of small cities and towns). During the period from 1960 to 1980, both the total population of the United States and those aged 60 and over have gravitated towards suburban locations and away from both central cities and small urban places. As is shown in table 3.2, the share of the urban elderly who resided in central cities declined from about half in 1960 to 42 percent in 1980; at the same time, the share of younger urbanites in central cities fell from 46 to 40 percent. During the same period, the share of elderly living in small towns diminished from one-fourth to one-fifth, while the share living in suburbs rose from 24 to 39 percent. Although trends are similar in these broad age groups, it should be noted that the tendency for the urban elderly to be less "suburbanized" than the younger urban population persists throughout this period.

There are fairly striking, yet changing, patterns in the age structure of the three types of urban areas. In 1960 and 1970, persons over the age of 75 were less likely to reside in central cities and suburbs than were younger elderly and, correspondingly, more likely to live in small urban places. In 1980, however, the older elderly became more likely than younger elderly to reside in central cities. If we put the trend in a slightly different way, we could argue that the mean age of central city elderly has begun to rise relative to that of other urban elderly. In 1960 and 1970, the mean age of central city elderly (69.9 and 70.6 years, respectively) was marginally less than that of all urban elderly (70.1 and 70.7 years, respectively); in 1980 the mean age of central city elderly increased to become slightly above that of all urban elderly (71.3 versus 71.2 years). The mean age among suburban elderly remains somewhat below (about one-half year) and the mean age of small town elderly remains somewhat above (also about one-half year) that of all older residents of urban areas.

The second aspect of population distribution that is of interest is the spatial component or the geographic structure of the older population. For sake of simplicity, the discussion will focus here upon the distribution of the older population in the four principal regions of the United States. These are illustrated in figure 3.1, while table 3.3 focuses on the distribution of the elderly between regions and the age structure of the elderly within each region. The first row of figures in table 3.3 shows the proportion of all persons in the United States who lived in each region at the time of the census. Basically, these data highlight the well-known regional shifts in population toward the South and, particularly, toward the West that have characterized the postwar period. In 1940, 43 percent of all Americans reside in these regions; by 1980, the proportion had increased to 52 percent. The latter year was, in fact, the first occasion when these two regions accounted for the majority of the nation's population. Increases in population share were much more pronounced in the West (11 to 19 percent) than in the South (32 to 33 percent). Conversely, the share of total popula-

Table 3.2
Persons Aged 60+ by Type of Urban Residence, United States,
1960-1980

Age	thousands of persons in:				percent in:		
	Urban	Central City	Suburbs	Other Urban	Central City	Suburbs	Other Urban
1980:							
Total	167051.0	67035.3	72135.4	27880.3	40.1%	43.2%	16.7%
60-64	7423.1	3002.1	3138.6	1282.4	40.4%	42.3%	17.3%
65-69	6423.6	2662.7	2544.3	1216.6	41.5%	39.6%	18.9%
70-74	5032.5	2113.1	1910.4	1009.0	42.0%	38.0%	20.0%
75-79	3613.9	1549.5	1318.3	746.1	42.9%	36.5%	20.6%
80-94	2249.4	963.1	908.2	478.1	42.8%	35.9%	21.3%
95+	1726.8	726.8	601.2	398.8	42.1%	34.8%	23.1%
[60+]	26469.3	11017.3	10321.0	5131.0	41.6%	39.0%	19.4%
[0-59]	140581.7	56018	61814.4	22749.3	39.8%	44.0%	16.2%

58

1970:

Total	149324.9	63921.7	54524.9	30878.3	42.8%	36.5%	20.7%
60-64	6238.5	2896.5	1994.1	1347.9	46.4%	32.0%	21.6%
65-69	5054.5	2390.3	1513.1	1151.1	47.3%	29.9%	22.8%
70-74	3981.3	1879.5	1165.4	936.4	47.2%	29.3%	23.5%
75-79	2813.2	1310.0	805.7	697.5	46.6%	28.6%	24.8%
80-84	1676.4	766.8	472.0	437.6	45.7%	28.2%	26.1%
85+	1105.7	495.5	307.6	302.6	44.8%	27.8%	27.4%
[60+]	20869.6	9738.6	6257.9	4873.1	46.7%	30.0%	23.4%
[0-59]	129455.3	54183.1	48267	26005.2	42.2%	37.6%	20.2%

1960:

Total	125268.8	57975.1	37873.4	29420.3	46.3%	30.2%	23.5%
60-64	5091.0	2616.1	1308.7	1166.2	51.4%	25.7%	22.9%
65-69	4402.4	2245.6	1079.0	1077.8	51.0%	24.5%	24.5%
70-74	3314.1	1662.9	786.0	865.2	50.2%	23.7%	26.1%
75-79	2100.9	1027.4	482.4	591.0	48.9%	23.0%	28.1%
80-84	1077.7	510.2	246.4	321.1	47.3%	22.9%	29.8%
85+	631.1	292.1	144.9	194.1	46.3%	23.0%	30.8%
[60+]	16617.1	8354.3	4047.4	4215.4	50.3%	24.4%	25.4%
[0-59]	108651.7	49620.8	33826	25204.9	45.7%	31.1%	23.2%

Source: Decennial Censuses of Population

Figure 3.1
Composition of U.S. Census Regions and Divisions

NORTHEAST REGION

    New England Division

- Connecticut
- Maine
- Massachusetts
- New Hampshire
- Rhode Island
- Vermont

    Middle Atlantic Division

- New Jersey
- New York
- Pennsylvania

MIDWEST REGION

    East North Central Division

- Illinois
- Indiana
- Michigan
- Ohio
- Wisconsin

    West North Central Division

- Iowa
- Kansas
- Minnesota
- Missouri
- Nebraska
- North Dakota
- South Dakota

SOUTH REGION

    South Atlantic Division

- Delaware
- District of Columbia
- Florida
- Georgia
- North Carolina
- South Carolina
- Virginia
- West Virginia

    East South Central Division

- Alabama
- Kentucky
- Mississippi
- Tennessee

    West South Central Division

- Arkansas
- Louisiana
- Oklahoma
- Texas

WEST REGION

    Mountain Division

- Arizona
- Colorado
- Idaho
- Montana
- New Mexico
- Utah
- Wyoming

    Pacific Division

- Alaska
- California
- Hawaii
- Oregon
- Washington

Source: U.S. Bureau of the Census.

Table 3.3
Regional Distribution of the Older Population, United States, 1940-1985

	1980				1970				1960			
	NE	MW	S	W	NE	MW	S	W	NE	MW	S	W
% of total	22%	26%	33%	19%	24%	28%	31%	17%	25%	29%	31%	16%
% of 60+	24%	26%	33%	17%	26%	28%	30%	15%	29%	30%	28%	14%
% of 60+/												
% of total	110%	100%	99%	90%	108%	101%	98%	91%	111%	106%	90%	92%
% of region aged 60+	17%	16%	16%	14%	15%	14%	14%	13%	15%	14%	12%	12%
% of persons aged 60+ who are:												
60-64	29%	28%	28%	29%	30%	29%	30%	30%	31%	30%	30%	30%
65-69	24%	24%	25%	25%	24%	24%	25%	24%	27%	26%	27%	26%
70-74	19%	19%	20%	19%	19%	19%	19%	19%	20%	20%	20%	20%
75-79	13%	14%	14%	13%	13%	14%	13%	13%	12%	13%	13%	13%
80-84	9%	9%	8%	8%	8%	9%	7%	8%	6%	7%	7%	7%
85+	6%	7%	6%	6%	5%	6%	5%	6%	4%	4%	4%	4%

Table 3.3 (continued)

	1950				1940*			
	NE	MW	S	W	NE	MW	S	W
% of total	26%	29%	31%	13%	27%	30%	32%	11%
% of 60+	28%	32%	26%	13%	29%	34%	26%	12%
% of 60+/ % of total	109%	110%	83%	100%	106%	110%	81%	111%
% of region aged 60+	13%	13%	10%	12%	11%	12%	8%	12%
% of persons aged 60+ who are:								
60-64	34%	33%	32%	33%	35%	33%	34%	35%
65-69	27%	27%	29%	27%	27%	27%	30%	27%
70-74	18%	19%	19%	19%	19%	19%	18%	19%
75-79	12%	12%	12%	11%	11%	12%	10%	11%
80-84	6%	6%	6%	6%	5%	6%	5%	6%
85+	3%	3%	3%	3%	2%	3%	3%	3%

	1985				1980			
	NE	MW	S	W	NE	MW	S	W
% of total	21%	25%	34%	20%	22%	26%	33%	19%
% of 65+	23%	26%	34%	18%	24%	26%	33%	17%
% of 65+/ % of total	110%	103%	99%	99%	110%	101%	100%	98%
% of region aged 65+	13%	12%	12%	11%	12%	11%	11%	10%
% of persons aged 65+ who are:								
65-74	59%	58%	60%	61%	60%	59%	63%	62%
75-84	31%	32%	31%	30%	31%	31%	30%	30%
85+	10%	10%	9%	9%	9%	10%	8%	9%

Sources: Decennial Censuses of Population
US Bureau of the Census, 1989a, p. 15-28

* - excludes Alaska and Hawaii

tion that resided in the Northeast and Midwest regions declined from 57 to 48 percent, with both regions experiencing substantial relative decline (in the Northeast from 27 to 22 percent; in the Midwest from 30 to 26 percent).

The regional redistribution of the older population has followed the same general trend as the redistribution of the entire population and, indeed, has been more salient. The share of persons aged 60 and over residing in the two northern regions stood at 63 percent in 1940 and declined gradually to marginally less than half (49.93 percent) in 1980. In other words, while their share of the total declined by about nine percentage points, their share of the elderly declined by thirteen points. The overall trend in these distributional changes can be seen quite easily in table 3.3 by following the index of redistribution (third line), which is simply the ratio of each region's share of the older population to that region's share of total population. A value of greater than 100 percent thus indicates a region with a larger share of the nation's elderly than of the nation's total population. In 1940, only the South had a disproportionately low share of elderly, with an index of only 81. This has increased markedly over the intervening four decades to the current level of approximate equality between shares of total and of elderly. This trend is in pronounced contrast to the experience in each of the other regions. In the West, the relative share of the elderly declined rapidly after World War II; this region is now appreciably younger than any other. For the Midwest, decline has been more gradual, but this region now, like the South, includes about the same share of the nation's elderly as it does other age groups. Only in the Northeast has the relative number of elderly remained more or less constant over time. Since 1960, this region has unequivocably had the largest relative share of American elderly.

Measured in terms of the share of regional population currently aged 60 and above (fourth line of table 3.3), each region has aged, but the process has occurred somewhat differently in each. In 1940, the proportion of the population aged 60 and over was 11 or 12 percent in each region except the South, where it was only 8 percent. Between 1940 and 1960, the rise in the share aged 60 and over was considerably more dramatic in the Northeast and South than elsewhere; by 1960, the Northeast, which had a lower share of elderly in 1940 than did either the Midwest or West, had become the oldest region. During this period, the South drew even with the West. Since 1960, the South has continued to age at a more rapid rate than any other region and, as of 1980, the share of the population aged 60 + was essentially identical at 16-17 percent in all regions save the West. In 1985, postcensal population estimates suggest that this same pattern persists, with 13 percent of the Northeast's population, 12 percent of that in the Midwest and South, and 11 percent of the West being aged at least 65 years.

Before we consider the role that variables such as migration and aging-in-place have played in effecting this regional redistribution, it would be appropriate to comment first on regional trends and differences in the age structure of the older population. Paralleling the national trends discussed previously, each region has seen substantial aging of its older population. In 1940, 60 to 64 percent of each region's older population was less than 70 years of age; by 1980, these portions had declined to a range of 52 to 54 percent. Among regions, there was variation in the extent of aging during the period. The West and Midwest regions, for example, each declined by eight percentage points (62 to 54 and 60 to 52, respectively), while the Northeast declined by nine (62 to 53) and the South by eleven (64 to 53). At the other end of the older age distribution, some 7 to 9 percent of the older population of each region was at least 80 years of age in 1940; this level increased without exception to levels of 14 to 16 percent in 1980. The Midwest has consistently had the largest share of oldest old within the ranks of its elderly; it has now been joined by the Northeast as more than 15 percent of the older population in each of these regions is aged 80 or over. Most of the diversity among regions in terms of the share aged 80 and over has emerged since 1960, when about 11 percent of the elderly in each region fell into this age category. During this most recent score of years, the share of elderly aged 80 + in the northern regions has increased by about five percentage points, in contrast to increases of only three percentage points in the South and West. During the five years subsequent to the 1980 census, this process has continued in all regions, especially in the South, where the share of the 65 + population aged 65 to 74 years declined from 63 to 60 percent.

These changes in the regional distribution of the older population are to some extent the result of regional differences in prior levels of fertility, mortality, and immigration but, in the main, reflect patterns of internal migration. Table 3.4 summarizes patterns of lifetime migration among persons aged 60 and over for

Table 3.4
Lifetime Migration Patterns of Persons Aged 60+, by Region of Current Residence,
United States, 1950-1980

Northeast in:

	Born and Living in Region	Net Migration to/from			
		Midwest	South	West	Total
1950	2,840,210	- 88,205	- 18,800	- 164,480	- 223,385
1960	3,621,334	- 76,311	- 48,909	- 208,932	- 334,052
1970	4,649,516	- 101,848	- 203,378	- 279,064	- 594,290
1990	6,236,758	- 145,226	- 616,480	- 491,813	- 1,253,519

Midwest in:

	Born and Living in Region	Net Migration to/from			
		Northeast	South	West	Total
1950	4,038,455	88,205	- 4,955	- 908,380	- 815,220
1960	5,018,042	76,311	- 29,220	- 1,180,675	- 1,075,144
1970	5,876,477	101,848	- 26,123	- 1,318,753	- 1,190,782
1990	7,198,682	145,226	- 10,833	- 1,740,314	- 1,605,921

South in:

	Northeast	Midwest	West	Total
1950	3,967,110	18,800	4,955	228,780	252,535
1960	5,129,819	48,909	29,220	362,274	342,595
1970	6,649,020	203,379	26,123	517,424	340,169
1980	8,093,289	616,480	10,833	776,246	148,933

West in:

	Northeast	Midwest	South	Total
1950	434,120	164,480	908,380	228,780	1,301,640
1960	752,498	208,832	1,180,675	362,274	1,751,781
1970	1,214,502	279,064	1,318,753	517,424	2,115,241
1980	1,970,485	491,813	1,740,314	776,246	3,008,373

Percent of Native Population Currently Residing in Region of Birth

	Northeast	Midwest	South	West	Total
1950	84.5%	74.5%	83.9%	92.9%	80.6%
1960	83.3%	73.2%	81.6%	93.1%	79.4%
1970	81.7%	73.3%	81.4%	92.6%	79.3%
1980	76.0%	70.3%	77.4%	89.7%	75.6%

Source: Decennial Censuses of Population

each census from 1950 to 1980. The data, which are restricted to persons born in the United States, show for each region the number of older persons born and currently residing in that region, as well as the net lifetime exchanges of older persons between that region and each additional region.

Corresponding to generally increasing numbers of births in the past and to successively lower levels of mortality at each age, in every region there is a clear and sustained increase in the size of the older population that was born in and that currently resides in the region of birth. These increases range from 78 percent in the Midwest to more than 350 percent in the West. However, for all regions, there has been a reduction in the proportion of the older population that continues to reside in the region of birth; these declines are most pronounced for the most recent intercensal period. There has also been some change in the relative degree of retention among regions. While the West has maintained its status as the "most retentive" region, the South has now surpassed the Northeast in this regard. The Midwest remains the least retentive region throughout the period.

In terms of the volume of lifetime migration, the two northern regions show continual increases in total net outmigration over time, while the West shows continual increases in total net inmigration. Lifetime net outmigration from the South increased during the 1950s, remained about constant during the 1960s, and declined dramatically during the 1970s, although the balance remains negative. In fact, throughout the period, the West is the only region with any lifetime net inmigration. These trends are illustrated in figure 3.2, which displays for each region the share of the native-born elderly born in and currently residing in that region for the years 1950 and 1980. While the share of the 60+ population born in the Northeast increased by a few percentage points over the interval, the share actually residing in the region remained perfectly constant. In the West, by way of contrast, both the proportion of the older population by place of birth and place of residence increased markedly, while in the Midwest, both proportions declined. Only in the South was there some degree of overall stability, with a marginal reduction in proportion born in the region and a marginal increase in the proportion currently resident.

During the 1970s, the volume of lifetime net outmigration increased substantially from both the Northeast and Midwest re-

Figure 3.2
Regional Distribution of Older Population by Place of Birth and Place of Residence, 1950 and 1980

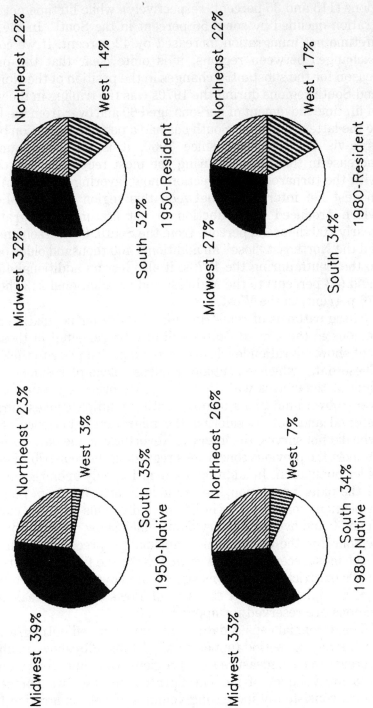

Source: U.S. Bureau of the Census, 1950 and 1980 Censuses of Population.

gions (115 and 35 percent, respectively), while lifetime net outmigration declined by some 56 percent in the South. In the West, lifetime net inmigration increased by 42 percent. If we consider exchanges between regions, it is quite clear that the primary reason for the substantial changes in the position of the Northeast and South regions during the 1970s was the tripling in the volume of lifetime movement of persons aged 60 and over from the former to the latter. While the South has had a positive migration balance vis-à-vis the Northeast since 1960, it is the large numerical increase in this balance during the most recent decade, coupled with the turnaround in direction (now favoring the South) in the modest net interchange between this region and the Midwest, which produced the reduction in net lifetime outmigration of nearly 200 thousand persons from the South. Conversely, not only did the Northeast "lose" an additional 400 thousand older persons to the South during the 1970s, it also lost an additional 45 thousand (43 percent) to the Midwest and an additional 213 thousand (76 percent) to the West.

These patterns of redistribution of the older population among regions in the United States will also be reflected in those data that show migration levels over a fixed period prior to the census. These data, which essentially contrast place of residence at the time of the census with that five years prior, are subject to the well-known limitations of not treating multiple moves during an interval and not considering the migration experience of those who did not survive the interval. Nevertheless, the data do serve to support the previous conclusions regarding the redistribution of the older population. In addition, by focusing only upon recent moves of the older population, we are able to abstract from residential relocations made earlier in life by individuals who are currently aged 60 and over. Summary data, which show net flows by age to regions for the quinquennia immediately preceding each of the three most recent censuses as well as for the first five years of the 1980s (restricted to persons aged 65 and over), are shown in table 3.5. Complete data on the size of flows between each pair of regions are reserved for appendices 5-8.

The decennial census data on inmigration and outmigration for each five-year period (upper panel of table 3.5) show an absolute increase in each measure for all regions over time, consistently increasing volumes of net outmigration for the two northern regions, consistently increasing volumes of net inmigration for the

Table 3.5
In, Out, and Net Migration, by Age and Region, United States, 1955-1960, 1965-1970, 1975-1980, and 1980-1985

(thousands of persons)

	1955 to 1960			1965 to 1970			1975 to 1980			1980 to 1985		
	In	Out	Net	In	Out	Net	In	Out	Net	In	Out	Net
Northeast												
60-64	13	51	-38	15	62	-47	17	122	-105			
65-69	12	57	-46	12	70	-53	16	121	-106			
70-74	9	36	-27	10	44	-34	12	70	-58			
75+	11	28	-17	15	42	-27	24	73	-50			
60+	45	172	-127	52	218	-165	68	386	-318			
65+	32	121	-89	38	155	-118	51	264	-213	49	181	-132
Midwest												
60-64	25	66	-41	26	75	-49	31	120	-89			
65-69	21	72	-51	23	77	-54	27	109	-81			
70-74	16	45	-30	17	46	-29	22	61	-39			
75+	19	39	-19	28	51	-23	41	71	-31			
60+	80	221	-141	94	249	-155	122	361	-239			
65+	55	156	-100	68	174	-106	90	241	-150	88	146	-58

Table 3.5 (continued)

(thousands of persons)

	1955 to 1960			1965 to 1970			1975 to 1980			1980 to 1985		
	In	Out	Net	In	Out	Net	In	Out	Net	In	Out	Net
South												
60-64	79	31	47	108	29	78	197	41	156			
65-69	90	24	66	114	25	89	188	36	152			
70-74	54	18	37	67	20	47	105	28	76			
75+	40	22	19	62	32	31	105	53	52			
60+	263	95	168	351	106	245	595	158	436			
65+	185	64	121	243	76	167	398	117	280	312	107	205
West												
60-64	48	16	32	43	25	18	74	37	37			
65-69	46	15	31	42	20	23	66	32	35			
70-74	30	11	20	29	13	15	41	20	20			
75+	29	11	17	37	17	19	57	28	28			
60+	153	53	100	151	76	75	238	117	121			
65+	105	37	68	108	50	57	164	80	83	80	95	-15

(percent of -period population)

	1955 to 1960			1965 to 1970			1975 to 1980			1980 to 1985		
	In	Out	Net	In	Out	Net	In	Out	Net	In	Out	Net
Northeast												
60-64	.7%	2.5%	-1.9%	.7%	2.8%	-2.1%	.7%	4.9%	-4.2%			
65-69	.7%	3.3%	-2.6%	.7%	3.9%	-3.2%	.7%	5.8%	-5.1%			
70-74	.7%	2.8%	-2.1%	.7%	3.0%	-2.3%	.7%	4.3%	-3.6%			
75+	.8%	2.0%	-1.2%	.8%	2.1%	-1.3%	1.0%	3.0%	-2.1%			
60+	.7%	2.7%	-2.0%	.7%	2.9%	-2.2%	.8%	4.5%	-3.7%			
65+	.7%	2.7%	-2.0%	.7%	3.0%	-2.3%	.8%	4.3%	-3.5%	.7%	2.7%	-2.0%

Midwest

60-64	1.2%	3.1%	-1.9%	1.1%	3.2%	-2.1%	1.2%	4.6%	-3.4%	
65-69	1.1%	3.9%	-2.7%	1.2%	4.0%	-2.8%	1.2%	4.8%	-3.6%	
70-74	1.1%	3.2%	-2.1%	1.1%	3.0%	-1.9%	1.3%	3.4%	-2.2%	
75+	1.1%	2.3%	-1.2%	1.2%	2.2%	-1.0%	1.5%	2.6%	-1.1%	
60+	1.1%	3.1%	-2.0%	1.2%	3.1%	-1.9%	1.3%	3.8%	-2.5%	1.2% 2.0%
65+	1.1%	3.1%	-2.0%	1.2%	3.0%	-1.8%	1.3%	3.6%	-2.2%	-.8%

South

60-64	4.0%	1.6%	2.4%	4.0%	1.1%	2.9%	5.9%	1.2%	4.7%	
65-69	5.2%	1.4%	3.3%	5.2%	1.1%	4.0%	6.2%	1.2%	5.1%	
70-74	4.3%	1.4%	2.9%	4.1%	1.2%	2.9%	4.4%	1.2%	3.2%	
75+	2.7%	1.5%	1.3%	2.8%	1.4%	1.4%	3.3%	1.7%	1.6%	
60+	4.1%	1.5%	2.6%	4.0%	1.2%	2.8%	5.0%	1.3%	3.7%	
65+	4.1%	1.4%	2.7%	4.0%	1.3%	2.8%	4.6%	1.4%	3.3%	3.2% 1.1% 2.1%

West

60-64	4.8%	1.6%	3.2%	3.2%	1.3%	4.1%	2.0%	2.1%		
65-69	5.2%	1.7%	3.5%	3.9%	2.1%	4.3%	2.1%	2.3%		
70-74	4.4%	1.6%	2.9%	3.5%	1.8%	3.5%	1.8%	1.8%		
75+	3.6%	1.4%	2.2%	3.0%	1.6%	3.4%	1.7%	1.7%		
60+	4.6%	1.6%	3.0%	3.4%	1.7%	3.9%	1.9%	2.0%		
65+	4.5%	1.6%	2.9%	3.5%	1.8%	4.9%	2.4%	2.5%	1.6% 1.9% -.3%	

Sources: Decennial Censuses of population
US Bureau of the Census, 1987, p. 39

South, and fluctuating, though always positive, levels for the West, with comparatively little overall change. If one considers levels of migration as a percentage of end-of-period population for each region (lower panel of table 3.5—note that these are not true rates), one may draw the following conclusions. Inmigration to the Northeast and Midwest regions has occurred at a more or less constant rate across all ages (within each region) and across time, although some increase in inmigration among those aged 75 and over might be noted in the most recent period. Outmigration "rates" in these regions tend to vary by age, with higher levels being observed among those who would most probably have retired from the labor force during the interval. Overall, these relative levels of outmigration were little changed from the first to the second interval but increased quite dramatically, particularly in the Northeast, between the second and third intervals. Consequently, in both regions, the overall level of net outmigration among the older population stood at about 2 percent of end-of-period population during both the late 1950s and late 1960s; however, by the late 1970s, this level had risen to nearly 4 percent for the Northeast and to 2.5 percent for the Midwest.

Trends in the South and West are, naturally, the mirror image of those occurring in the northern regions. This fact is particularly true of the South, which, between 1975 and 1980, received nearly three times the number of older movers from the North than did the West. Relative inmigration levels to the South were quite unchanged for the two initial periods but rose markedly in the third. Outmigration rates declined somewhat between the first two periods but remained more or less fixed thereafter, with the exception of some increase in outmigration among the very old. This trend of course parallels the observed increase in inmigration among the very old in the northern regions and may suggest an increase in the level of return migration among persons who had previously moved to the South upon retirement ten or more years previously (Litwak and Longino, 1987; Serow and Charity, 1988). For the West, inmigration behaved somewhat erratically, decreasing across all ages from the first to the second period, then increasing across all ages from the second to the third. Relative levels of outmigration among the elderly from the West have tended to increase over time. As a result of the differing trends for inmigration and outmigration, net migration of the elderly to the South has increased in proportion over time, albeit to a much greater extent during the last quinquennium, when it rose from nearly 3 to nearly 4 percent of the end-of-period population. Conversely, elderly net migration to the West declined in relative terms by nearly half between 1955-60 and 1965-70 and has increased only modestly since. To a large and perhaps increasing extent, the recent redistribution of the older population through migration is centered upon the South region; this trend largely, but not entirely, reflects the presence of the state of Florida in this region. For example, between 1975 and 1980 some 1.7 million Americans who were at least 60 years of age (in 1980) changed their state of residence; of these, some 429 thousand (26 percent) relocated to Florida. By way of contrast, only 6 percent of the 35.6 million older Americans enumerated in the 1980 census lived in Florida.

Data for the period subsequent to 1980, from the Current Population Survey, suggest that the volume of population redistribution among those over the age of 65 has slowed in recent years. A pronounced decline in outmigration from the North, coupled with approximately constant elderly inflows to these regions, has led to sharp reductions in the volume and rate of net outmigration, relative to the 1975-80 period. These declines, in turn, have led to declines in the volume of inmigration to the South and, in particular, to the West, where the level was nominally negative, though not (statistically) significantly different from zero. Thus the redistribution of the older American population is now entirely directed toward the South, on balance. The results of the 1990 census will go far in establishing whether the results of the early 1980s are, in fact, the beginnings of a trend slowdown or reversal, or simply a consequence of the relatively small sample size of the Current Population Survey.

Prior to concluding our discussion on migration behavior of the elderly in the United States, it seems appropriate to offer a few comments on the observed relationship between residential mobility and age. As a general statement, it seems fair to say that residential mobility is most often considered as a phenomenon of the young. Model migration schedules show pronounced regularity in age-specific patterns of movement, with a peak around age 25 and gradual decline thereafter. There is often, but not always, a secondary peak around the age of retirement (Rogers and Castro, 1981). Much of our knowledge of migration among the elderly is flawed by an excessive level of aggregation that precludes analysis

Figure 3.3
Share of Population Moving by Age and Distance, 1975-1980

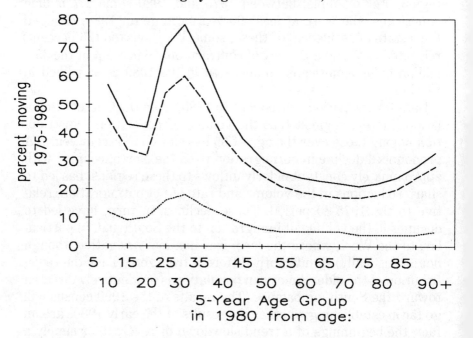

LEGEND
_____ Total
_ _ _ . Intrastate
.... Interstate

Source: U.S. Bureau of the Census, 1980 Census of Population.

of age differentiation in elderly mobilty. There can be no question that mobility for the United States during the period 1975 to 1980 conformed to the general model: mobility rates were at a maximum among persons aged 25-29 in 1980 and declined thereafter. Slightly more than half those aged 5 to 54 in 1980 had moved at least once during the prior five years; this was true for slightly less than one-fourth of those aged 55 or over. However, with greater disaggregation, it becomes clear that residential mobility actually increases with age among the older population. As shown in figure 3.3, the share of the population that had moved declined from 23 percent for those in their early 60s to about 21 percent for those in their 70s, but then rose steadily, reaching a level of more than 30 percent among those at least 90 years of age.

Although the reason for this phenomenon is not perfectly understood, it probably lies in our increased understanding that mobility of older persons is not a unidimensional phenomenon associated with amenity seeking upon retirement. Rather, it is closely tied to life course occurrences wherein retirement, bereavement, and failing health could intervene at different stages of the elderly life course to stimulate residential mobility. Thus, one might expect to see amenity migration among "young-old" couples, but support- or care-seeking migration among "old-old" widowed (Litwak and Longino, 1987). Additionally, it might be conjectured that origin-destination patterns would differ according to type of move: from North to South for the young-old, but, perhaps increasingly, from South to North for the old-old.

4

FAMILY, HOUSEHOLD, AND HOUSING CHARACTERISTICS

Age and gender differences in mortality as well as rates and patterns of remarriage strongly suggest that patterns of marital composition be examined separately by gender. The extent to which these factors operate is clearly revealed in table 4.1, where recent changes in the marital status of the elderly can be traced. In 1940, more than two-thirds of all males aged 60 and over were married; this proportion increased quite steadily to nearly 80 percent by 1980. Among all older females, there has been almost no change in proportion currently married, with the level increasing only from 42 to 45 percent. Similarly, the share of older women who were widowed has changed but little, declining from 48 percent in 1940 to 44 percent in 1980. On the other hand, the prevalence of widowhood among older men diminished from 20 to 12 percent.

There is an inverse relationship between age and the percent currently married as well as a direct relationship between age and the percent widowed for each gender at each point in time. Among males in 1940, the percent married ranged from 77 percent among those aged 60-64 to 33 percent among those at least 85; for females the comparable proportions were 58 and 7 percent, respectively. Between 1940 and 1980, the percent of males currently married at each specific age increased, but by absolutely and relatively more at the upper end of the elderly age spectrum. Hence, the overall differential of forty-four percentage points observed in 1940 was

Table 4.1
Marital Status, by Age and Gender, United States, 1940-1987

(percent distribution)

	MALE				FEMALE			
	Never Married	Married	Widowed	Divorced	Never Married	Married	Widowed	Divorced
60 to 64								
1987	NA	NA	NA	NA	NA	NA	NA	NA
1980	5.2%	85.2%	4.6%	5.0%	5.2%	65.7%	22.6%	6.5%
1970	6.6%	84.6%	5.2%	3.6%	7.2%	63.1%	24.9%	4.8%
1960	7.7%	82.8%	6.5%	3.0%	7.7%	61.4%	27.6%	3.3%
1950	8.6%	79.3%	9.6%	2.5%	8.2%	60.0%	29.7%	2.1%
1940	10.5%	76.7%	11.1%	1.7%	9.3%	58.0%	31.3%	1.4%
65 to 74								
1987	4.7%	81.5%	9.0%	4.8%	4.8%	53.0%	36.7%	5.5%
1980	5.4%	81.6%	8.9%	4.1%	6.2%	49.4%	39.3%	5.1%
1970	7.2%	78.6%	10.9%	3.3%	7.6%	46.6%	42.0%	3.8%
1960	7.7%	76.7%	13.0%	2.6%	8.1%	46.2%	43.3%	2.4%
1950	9.6%	71.4%	17.3%	2.1%	9.7%	43.9%	46.1%	1.3%
1940	10.1%	69.1%	19.3%	1.5%	9.4%	41.6%	48.1%	.9%

75 to 94

1987*	4.3%	68.8%	23.6%	3.2%	6.4%	23.8%	67.0%	2.7%
1980	5.7%	70.3%	21.0%	3.0%	7.1%	24.9%	64.8%	3.2%
1970	7.4%	65.0%	25.0%	2.6%	8.5%	23.8%	65.2%	2.5%
1960	7.8%	61.1%	29.2%	1.9%	9.1%	23.5%	66.0%	1.4%
1950	7.8%	55.4%	35.4%	1.4%	9.4%	21.0%	68.9%	.6%
1940	9.3%	53.0%	37.3%	.3%	9.1%	19.7%	70.8%	.4%

85+

1987	NA	NA	NA	NA	NA	NA	NA	NA
1980	5.6%	48.4%	43.8%	2.1%	7.9%	8.4%	81.8%	2.0%
1970	10.8%	43.4%	43.4%	2.4%	10.7%	10.8%	76.8%	1.7%
1960	7.1%	38.7%	52.8%	1.4%	9.6%	8.2%	81.4%	.8%
1950	7.7%	33.6%	57.9%	.8%	9.7%	7.0%	82.9%	.4%
1940	7.9%	33.0%	58.5%	.6%	8.0%	6.7%	85.1%	.2%

60+

1987	NA	NA	NA	NA	NA	NA	NA	NA
1980	5.4%	79.0%	11.5%	4.1%	6.3%	44.8%	44.1%	4.3%
1970	7.2%	76.3%	13.2%	3.2%	7.9%	44.0%	44.5%	3.7%
1960	7.7%	74.5%	15.3%	2.6%	9.3%	44.3%	45.0%	2.4%
1950	8.4%	70.4%	19.1%	2.1%	8.7%	43.4%	46.5%	1.4%
1940	10.1%	68.4%	20.2%	1.4%	9.3%	42.3%	47.5%	1.0%

Sources: Decennial Censuses of Population
US Bureau of the Census, 1988b, p. 3-8

* - 1987 data are for persons aged 75 and over

81

reduced to thirty-seven points in 1980. Among females, changes at each age are smaller than among males and are not nearly so different by age. Consequently, the differential between the youngest and oldest age segments for women actually widened, from fifty-one to fifty-seven percentage points.

With this knowledge in hand, the outcome of differentials in the share widowed by age is quite obvious. The difference for males was about forty-eight percentage points in 1940; this level fell to thirty-nine points in 1980. For females, the observed initial differential of fifty-four points widened to almost sixty by the time of the most recent census. Finally, for both genders, across all ages, and for each point in time, some 10 percent of the population was either single (never married) or divorced. In general, the proportion in the former state has diminished over time, while the share divorced has risen. There are also consistent age differences, with divorce being more prevalent among the younger elderly regardless of gender or time period. Data from the Current Population Survey show quite pronounced increases in the share divorced, especially among those aged 65 to 74.

Data on living arrangements are particularly useful in that they provide information on the environment in which the elderly function on a daily basis. Compiling historical series of data on living arrangements, even for the short period of time under consideration here (that is, from 1940 to 1980), is difficult because of changes in tabulating procedures and changes in concepts such as the recent transition from "head of household" (always an adult male if present) to "householder" (the person in whose name the dwelling unit is owned or rented) for the 1980 census. Nevertheless, it is possible to identify how each person in a household relates to the head or householder in rather broad terms; these data are presented in table 4.2. Again, for reasons largely similar to those identified under the rubric "marital status," it is vital to consider gender-specific changes in living arrangements.

In 1940, more than 95 percent of all men aged 60 and over lived in households; a large majority (more than 80 percent) of these were household heads. About 12 percent lived in a household headed by a child or other relative, and the remaining 6 percent lived in a household headed by a nonrelative. The proportion heading households rose during each intercensal period until the most recent, when the concept of householder was introduced. While the number of household heads among all older males accounted for

Table 4.2
Relationship to Head of Household, by Age and Gender, United
States, 1940-1980

(percent distribution)

	Head	Spouse	Other Relative	Non-Relative	Group Quarters	Total (000s)
MALE						
60 to 64						
1980	91.0%	3.2%	3.2%	1.3%	1.3%	4,695
1970	93.1%	0.0%	3.6%	1.4%	1.9%	4,044
1960	89.8%	0.0%	5.0%	2.3%	2.9%	3,384
1950	84.2%	0.0%	6.2%	4.1%	5.5%	2,982
1940	83.5%	0.0%	6.9%	5.4%	4.2%	2,398
65 to 74						
1980	89.7%	3.3%	3.7%	1.2%	2.1%	6,740
1970	91.0%	0.0%	4.8%	1.6%	2.6%	5,433
1960	87.1%	0.0%	7.1%	2.5%	3.3%	5,022
1950	80.2%	0.0%	9.8%	4.4%	5.6%	4,007
1940	79.5%	0.0%	10.7%	5.5%	4.2%	3,167

Table 4.2 (continued)

(percent distribution)

	Head	Spouse	Other Relative	Non-Relative	Group Quarters	Total (000s)
MALE						
75+						
1980	80.1%	3.2%	7.6%	1.3%	7.8%	3,522
1970	79.3%	0.0%	11.2%	2.0%	7.4%	3,005
1960	73.7%	0.0%	16.3%	3.0%	7.0%	2,287
1950	65.9%	0.0%	21.6%	4.7%	7.8%	1,727
1940	65.1%	0.0%	23.3%	6.0%	5.7%	1,239
60+						
1980	87.9%	3.2%	4.5%	1.3%	3.2%	14,957
1970	88.9%	0.0%	5.9%	1.7%	3.5%	12,482
1960	85.0%	0.0%	8.4%	2.5%	4.0%	10,694
1950	78.8%	0.0%	10.9%	4.4%	6.0%	8,717
1940	78.3%	0.0%	11.7%	5.5%	4.5%	6,804
FEMALE						
60 to 64						
1980	32.4%	59.8%	5.7%	1.0%	1.1%	5,440
1970	29.7%	59.1%	8.1%	1.5%	1.5%	4,607
1960	27.0%	57.2%	11.6%	2.1%	2.1%	3,727
1950	23.5%	54.6%	14.9%	3.5%	3.4%	3,029
1940	24.7%	52.7%	15.6%	4.4%	2.6%	2,330

65 to 74					
1980	44.4%	44.3%	8.0%	1.0%	2.3%	8,850
1970	40.6%	43.0%	12.1%	1.5%	2.7%	7,007
1960	35.1%	42.2%	17.5%	2.2%	3.0%	5,926
1950	30.8%	39.3%	22.4%	4.0%	4.0%	4,398
1940	31.9%	36.6%	23.9%	4.6%	3.0%	3,209
75+					
1980	52.2%	17.3%	16.0%	1.0%	13.4%	6,386
1970	44.8%	18.2%	23.6%	1.7%	11.8%	4,658
1960	38.5%	17.6%	31.8%	2.8%	9.3%	3,073
1950	33.8%	14.9%	38.9%	4.4%	8.0%	2,125
1940	34.7%	14.0%	41.1%	5.1%	5.1%	1,404
60+					
1980	43.7%	40.0%	9.9%	1.0%	5.4%	20,676
1970	38.7%	40.5%	14.3%	1.5%	5.0%	16,272
1960	33.6%	40.5%	19.3%	2.3%	4.3%	12,626
1950	28.9%	38.1%	23.5%	3.9%	4.7%	9,551
1940	30.0%	37.5%	24.6%	4.6%	3.3%	6,944

Source: Decennial Censuses of Population

89 percent of this population in 1970, the decline to 88 percent in 1980 was minimal. The inclusion of an additional 3 percent of older males as spouses of the householder at this time suggests that a level of 91 percent classified as "head of household" would be approximately consistent with the pre-1980 definition. The share of older males living in households headed by relatives other than spouse or by nonrelatives has declined steadily over time and stood at 5 and 1 percent of the household population, respectively, in 1980. In summary, the dominant trend among older males in households has been a successive increase in the share heading their own household or (in 1980) married to the head. Conversely, the shares in other household living arrangements diminished steadily over time. Indeed, this latter trend is so pronounced that it is not only the relative numbers that have declined for each of the other two household categories, the absolute number of older males in the category was lower in 1980 than in 1940, despite the overall increase of 120 percent in the number of males aged 60 or more years.

A generally similar pattern can be observed for females aged 60 and over; the number of heads/householders increased from 2.1 million in 1940 to slightly more than 9 million in 1980. As a share of all females in households, the relative number of heads rose from 31 to 46 percent. The proportion of older women who were classified as spouse of the head has, by way of contrast, been quite stable over the entire period, increasing only from 38 to 40 percent. As was the case for older men, the share of older women residing in a household headed by a nonspousal relative or by some other person was considerably reduced, from about one-third of the 1940 household population to only slightly more than one-tenth by 1980.

As would be expected, there are pronounced differences in the living arrangements of older persons according to their current age. Although the gender-specific trends described in the preceding paragraphs apply equally well to all ages, the overall levels for each type of living arrangement vary quite consistently with age: with increased age, there is a diminished tendency to be the head of household and a correspondingly increased tendency to reside in the household of a nonspousal relative. This tendency is most evident at the oldest ages. In the majority of these instances, the nonspousal relative is a child. It is perhaps particularly noteworthy to consider the general decreasing tendency of the very old to reside with relatives in light of the generally increasing tendency for this population to reside in "group quarters," which for persons in this age group almost always means a nursing home or some other long-term care arrangement. These divergent tendencies are clearly illustrated in figure 4.1, which presents for persons aged 85 and over the shares that lived with a child and that lived in an institution from 1950 to 1980.

The share of oldest old men living with one of their children has declined from more than a fourth of the population in 1950 to less than 10 percent in 1980. At the same time, the share residing in institutions rose from 12 to 17 percent. Changes among oldest old women were even more striking. In 1950, more than 41 percent of women aged 85 or over resided with a child; this form of living arrangement was the most common one for women of this age until after 1960. This trend has fallen quite rapidly since and in 1980 only included 13 percent of very old women. Conversely, the share of women at least 85 years old that resides in a nursing home (or similar environment) now stands at more than one-fourth. In a very real sense, it must be noted that it appears that the primary locus of care for the very old has shifted during the past few decades from the family to institutions. Because much of the cost associated with this institutional care is ultimately met by public funds through Medicaid, it could also be argued that much of the real responsibility for the care of the oldest old has shifted from the family to the public sector. As will be discussed at the end of this book, the projected growth of the very old population, in conjunction with this shift in financial responsibility for care, could have profound economic implications.

Among the most significant outcomes of the changes in both marital status and living arrangements of the elderly is the increased tendency among them to live alone. As is shown in table 4.3, the proportion of older persons, regardless of age or gender, who live alone increased by more than one-third between 1960 and 1980. Increases were much greater among females (43 percent) than among males (9 percent) and increased steadily with age, from 12 percent for those in their early 60s to more than 84 percent among those over 85. In absolute numbers, the number of older persons living alone more than doubled, from 4.1 to 8.6 million; of the increase of 4.5 million, some 1.6 million, or 36 percent, were aged 75 to 84, and an additional half million, or 11 percent, were at least 85 years of age.

Figure 4.1
Proportion of Persons Aged 85+ Living with a Child or in an Institution, by Gender, 1950-1980

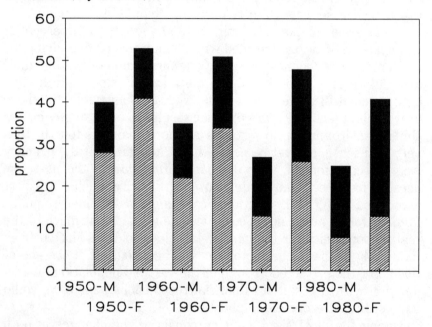

LEGEND
- ■ In Institution
- ▨ With Child

Source: U.S. Bureau of the Census, 1950-1980 Censuses of Population.

Table 4.3
Proportion of Noninstitutionalized Elderly Living Alone, by Age
and Gender, United States, 1960-1980

	1960	1970	1980	Percent Change
MALE:				
60-64	8.7	9.6	9.1	4.6%
65-74	11.8	13.8	12.1	2.5%
75-84	16.6	20.2	18.8	13.3%
85+	17.7	23.0	26.1	47.5%
60+	11.8	14.0	12.9	9.2%
FEMALE:				
60-64	18.2	21.7	20.9	14.8%
65-74	25.5	33.1	34.2	34.1%

Table 4.3 (continued)

	1960	1970	1980	Percent Change
FEMALE:				
75-84	30.6	42.0	48.8	59.5%
85+	23.8	33.7	46.1	93.7%
60+	24.2	31.7	34.5	42.5%
TOTAL:				
60-64	13.7	16.1	15.4	12.7%
65-74	19.2	24.7	24.6	28.5%
75-84	24.5	33.1	37.4	53.1%
85+	21.4	29.6	39.4	84.4%
60+	18.5	24.0	25.3	36.7%

Source: Decennial Censuses of Population

What is frequently very important for the social, economic, physical, and psychological well-being of older persons living alone, especially those who would be categorized as being very old, is the proximity of friends or relatives to provide care and support. Unfortunately, census data in the United States do not provide any information of this sort, except in those instances where the older person shares a household with such relatives or friends. Figure 4.2 displays aggregate-level estimates of the mean number of children ever born and the mean number of children surviving to the age of 60 for past, current, and future cohorts of older women as they attain the age of 85. While the number of children ever born declines rapidly for cohorts reaching 85 after 1955 and until the turn of the next century, the number of surviving children does not decline nearly so much. This fact is the result of the reduced levels of mortality at younger ages discussed earlier in this book. While the number of children ever born will decline by 40 percent among women attaining age 85 between 1991 and 1995, compared to those reaching this age between 1956 and 1960, the average number of children surviving to age 60 will decline by only 16 percent. For all later cohorts, mean levels of both children ever born and, more importantly, surviving children increase (although not constantly) over time. On average, then, each oldest old female will have, on average, one and one-half to two and one-half living children when she reaches the age of 85. In short, while lowered fertility reduces the pool of potential caregivers for the very old, this reduction is partially offset by the more favorable mortality experience of the children of future old old cohorts.

The final topic to be considered within this chapter is the characteristics of the elderly in the United States with regard to housing. The focus here will largely be on issues of tenure (that is, whether the individuals own or rent the house or flat in which they reside) and their housing costs relative to levels of income. In addition, some brief mention will be made regarding characteristics of the housing units themselves, with regard to the age of the unit and amenities available in it. Summary housing data for the year 1980 are provided in table 4.4. The data that are included in this section are largely adapted from those presented in a recent study by Griffith (1985). Older males who head their own household are somewhat more likely than older female heads not only to own the housing unit they inhabit (72 and 67 percent, respectively), but

Figure 4.2
Estimated Average Number of Children Ever Born and Children
Surviving to Age 60, Female Cohorts Reaching Age 85, 1956-2025

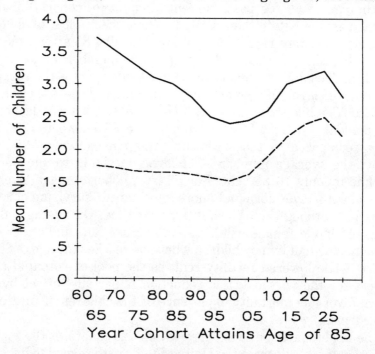

LEGEND

———— Ever Born

– – – – Surviving to Age 60

Source: U.S. Bureau of the Census, 1950-1980 Censuses of Population.

also to own it free of any debt to a lending institution (79 percent of male owners as opposed to 73 percent of female owners). In general, the probability that an older householder will own the unit in which (s)he resides decreases with age: only about one-fourth of those aged 60-64 rent their home, compared with nearly 40 percent of those over the age of 80. This tendency persists until the present, as shown by the Current Population Survey data presented at the bottom of table 4.4. However, among homeowners, the probability that the home is owned free of any mortgage obligation increases with age: at ages 80 and over, about 80 percent of owners are mortgage free, compared with only 60 percent among those 60 to 64 years of age. For many of the elderly, particularly the oldest old, it is very likely that the equity in an owner-occupied home is the single largest asset they possess. However, housing equity is notoriously illiquid, except upon the sale of the unit. It has been suggested (Chen and Scholen, 1980) that older individuals be able to convert some of their equity into cash and retain possession of their home while they remain alive (so-called reverse annuity mortgages), but this option has not become widely available as yet.

The importance of the latter issue is clarified by the four columns in table 4.4 that show the average share of older households' income that is expended for housing costs (these include rent, mortgage principal and interest payments, home insurance, and utilities). Because income is generally higher for older males than for older females and because it is inversely related to age within the older population, housing costs generally represent a larger share of income for female and older householders than they do for male and younger householders. Housing costs account for less than 13 percent of income in those households headed by men in their early 60s, but for more than twice this proportion in households headed by women aged 85 or over. For all American households, housing costs represented some 20.3 percent of total income, a figure slightly below the 20.9 percent of income among older households.

Summary indicators pertaining to the quality of the housing occupied by older persons are given in figures 4.3 and 4.4. Figure 4.3 shows the distribution by year built of housing units occupied by younger (head under age 60) and older households. As might be expected, older households generally reside in comparatively old units: half of all houses occupied by older households were at least

Table 4.4
Housing Characteristics of the Elderly, by Age and Gender, United States,
1980 and 1987

	Percent who:			Housing costs as % of income				Mean
1980: Male:	Rent	Own with mortgage	Own without mortgage	Renter	Own with mortgage	Own without mortgage	Total	Age of Unit
60-64	21.9%	33.7%	44.4%	17.8%	15.6%	8.1%	12.8%	26
65-69	24.1%	22.7%	53.2%	21.7%	20.5%	10.9%	15.7%	28
70-74	26.8%	16.0%	57.3%	23.5%	24.0%	12.5%	17.3%	30
75-79	30.3%	12.3%	57.5%	24.6%	27.6%	13.5%	18.6%	32
80-84	32.7%	10.6%	56.7%	25.5%	30.5%	14.6%	19.8%	35
85+	32.8%	12.2%	55.0%	25.8%	33.0%	15.6%	21.1%	38
60+	28.1%	14.8%	57.1%	21.9%	19.6%	12.4%	16.1%	29
Female:								
60-64	26.9%	26.0%	47.1%	27.2%	26.1%	14.6%	21.0%	29
65-69	31.0%	18.1%	50.9%	29.8%	33.1%	17.5%	24.1%	31
70-74	35.3%	13.7%	50.9%	30.8%	36.5%	19.1%	25.6%	32
75-79	39.6%	11.9%	48.5%	31.4%	37.4%	20.5%	26.8%	34
80-84	41.5%	11.9%	46.6%	31.7%	38.4%	21.6%	27.8%	36
85+	39.3%	13.4%	47.2%	31.8%	39.3%	22.3%	28.3%	> 41
60+	33.3%	17.7%	48.9%	30.0%	31.8%	18.1%	24.5%	32

Total:

60-64	24.6%	29.6%	45.8%	23.4%	20.6%	11.7%	17.2%	28
65-69	28.0%	20.1%	51.9%	26.8%	26.9%	14.5%	20.5%	30
70-74	31.8%	14.6%	53.5%	28.3%	30.9%	16.2%	22.2%	31
75-79	36.1%	12.0%	51.9%	29.2%	33.6%	17.6%	23.7%	33
80-84	38.4%	11.5%	50.1%	29.9%	35.9%	18.9%	25.1%	36
85+	37.2%	13.0%	49.8%	30.1%	37.4%	19.9%	26.0%	41
60+	31.2%	16.5%	52.4%	27.2%	26.0%	15.6%	20.9%	31

1987, Total

	Rent	Own
65-74	21.9%	78.1%
75+	29.3%	70.7%
65+	24.9%	75.1%

Sources: Griffith, 1985, p. 46-47
US Bureau of the Census, 1988a, p. 7

95

Figure 4.3
Age of Housing Unit by Age of Householder, 1980

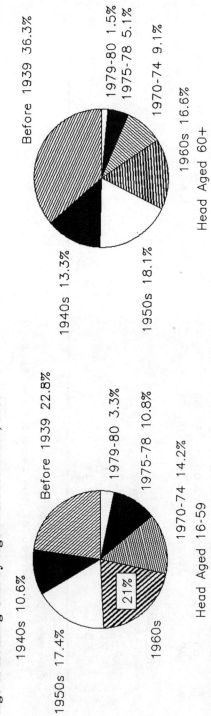

Source: U.S. Bureau of the Census, 1950-1980 Censuses of Population.

Figure 4.4
Absence of Selected Housing Amenities by Age and Gender
of Householder, United States, 1980

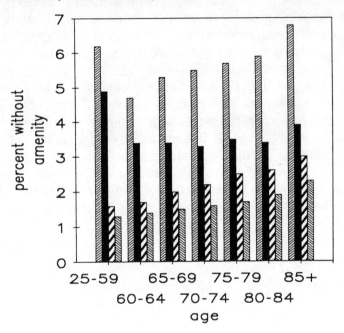

LEGEND
 Without Phone-Male
■ Without Phone-Female
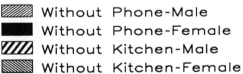 Without Kitchen-Male
▨ Without Kitchen-Female

Source: U.S. Bureau of the Census, 1980 Census of Housing.

thirty years old in 1980, compared with only one-third of the homes occupied by younger households. Conversely, the 30 percent of units occupied by young households that were less than ten years old is twice the proportion of new homes occupied by the elderly. While age of the structure is not, in and of itself, a perfect indicator of housing quality, it is generally correlated with the availability of modern conveniences and amenities. As suggested by figure 4.4, homes occupied by the elderly are somewhat less likely than those occupied by younger households to have complete kitchen facilities available (a set of structural characteristics which includes a sink with piped water, a stove, and a refrigerator). One may also note (not shown in the illustration) that the units occupied by older households were slightly less likely than those occupied by younger households to have complete lavatory facilities (flush toilet, piped hot water, tub or shower): 3 percent of houses occupied by older persons lacked either some or all of these amenities for their exclusive use, in contrast to only 2 percent of homes with a younger head of household. This age difference is not to be found for the availability of a telephone in the house, however. This latter amenity is, it should be noted, a matter of choice, rather than a structural characteristic of the dwelling unit.

5

SOCIAL AND ECONOMIC CHARACTERISTICS

This chapter deals with three distinct aspects of the socio-economic status of older persons in the United States: labor force, educational attainment, and levels of income and the incidence of poverty. Because labor force participation among older persons is so closely tied to the regulations governing eligibility for the receipt of pensions, it seems appropriate at this juncture to digress slightly and include a summary of the principal features of the publicly funded retirement system in the United States, namely the retirement program of the Social Security system.

Almost all workers in the United States now come under the aegis of Social Security. The primary exceptions are employees of state and local government entities with their own retirement system, federal civilian employees hired prior to January 1, 1984, certain student occupations, and those whose annual earnings are less than the minimum for coverage ($100 to $400, depending upon the nature of work). Self-employed persons must participate in the system if their net annual earnings exceed $400. At present, a total of 15.02 percent of annual earnings (to a maximum of $45,000) is paid by each worker; those who are not self-employed pay half this sum in the form of deductions made by the employer from gross earnings with the remainder paid directly by the employer. In order to be fully insured by the system, workers must have completed a minimum number of lifetime quarter-years of work, with a minimum level of earnings depending upon the calendar years in which the work was performed. The number of lifetime quarters of work needed for eligibility depends upon year of birth: persons born prior to 1918 require twenty-eight quarters, and persons born subsequent to 1928 require forty quarters. At present, minimum quarterly earnings required for full coverage is $470.

Persons may begin to claim retirement benefits as early as age 62, but the amount of the monthly benefit is reduced depending upon the difference between the actual age at retirement and the age at which one is eligible for full benefits. The level of benefits is dependent upon the level of earnings for each individual, relative to average wages among all workers in each year worked. The extent to which retirement benefits "replace" the level of earnings is an inverse function of earnings. For workers retiring in 1988, Social Security benefits would amount to 44 percent of wages among those who had earned $15,000 immediately prior to retirement, but only 23 percent for those with earnings of $45,000. The age of eligibility for full benefits is now set at 65 years for individuals born in 1937 or earlier but increases to 67 years for those persons born in 1960 or later. Similarly, by continuing to work after the attainment of the age of full eligibility, one may increase the monthly benefit level to be received upon retirement. A person eligible for benefits may receive benefits and continue to work. However, for persons under the age of 70, monthly benefits are reduced by $1 for every $2 earned if the worker earns more than $6,120 (if under age 65) or $8,400 (if aged 65 to 69) (The Hay Group, 1988).

As can be seen from table 5.1, labor force participation rates among older American males have declined dramatically from 1940 through 1980 and are projected to decline still further during the remainder of the present century. Labor force participation among men in their early 60s (that is, before the current age of eligibility for full Social Security retirement benefits) declined by about one-fourth between 1940 and 1980 and is projected to decline by about another 10 percent by 2000. For those who have attained the age of full eligibility, labor force participation rates in 1980 were about half the corresponding levels of 1940, with additional declines (especially among those in their late 60s) forecast for the duration of the century. Altogether, somewhat more than half of older men were engaged in the American labor force in

Table 5.1
Labor Force Participation Rates of Persons Aged 60+, by Age
and Gender, United States, 1940-2000

	1940	1950	1960	1970	1980	1990	2000
Male:							
60-64	79%	79%	78%	73%	60%	56%	53%
65-69	59%	60%	44%	39%	29%	23%	20%
70-74	38%	39%	29%	22%	18%	17%	15%
75-79	NA	24%	20%	14%	NA	NA	NA
80-84	NA	13%	12%	9%	NA	NA	NA
85+	NA	7%	7%	10%	NA	NA	NA
75+	18%	19%	15%	12%	9%	7%	6%
60+	55%	55%	45%	40%	32%	27%	23%
Female:							
60-64	14%	20%	29%	36%	34%	34%	34%
65-69	9%	13%	17%	17%	15%	14%	14%
70-74	5%	7%	10%	9%	8%	7%	6%
75-79	NA	4%	6%	6%	NA	NA	NA
80-84	NA	2%	3%	4%	NA	NA	NA
85+	NA	1%	2%	5%	NA	NA	NA
75+	2%	3%	4%	5%	3%	2%	2%
60+	9%	12%	16%	17%	15%	13%	12%

Source: US Senate, 1988, p. 90-91

1940; by 1980 this fraction had fallen to about one-third and is pro-jected to fall further, to less than one-quarter, at the turn of the twenty-first century.

The historical experience of older American women is quite the opposite, with labor force participation doubling between 1940 and 1980 for women aged 60 to 64 and increasing by more than 60 percent among other women under the age of 75. The absolute level of older female labor force participation remains much below that of older males but has risen appreciably over time: in 1940, the labor force participation rate of all women aged 60 and over was one-sixth that of similarly aged males; by 1980 the rate among women was almost half the male rate and would have exceeded this level had not the older female population experienced more rapid aging than the male during this interval. It would seem, however, that any substantial increase in labor force participation among older women is about over. The most recent labor force es-timates currently available (those for 1986) suggest that age-specific rates are at or slightly below those of 1980, and current projections suggest that this "flatness" in labor force participa-tion among older women will persist until at least the year 2000 (U.S. Senate, 1988).

In addition to observable changes in the extent to which older workers participate in the labor force, one may note considerable change in the extent to which older persons work full-time (de-fined as usually working thirty-five or more hours per week) as op-posed to part-time. For workers in their early 60s, there was little change between 1960 and 1980 in the share working full-time: about 90 percent of all economically active males and about 70 per-cent of all economically active females usually worked at least thirty-five hours per week in each year. At older ages, though, there were substantial increases in the relative numbers of part-time workers. For workers aged 65 to 69, the share of part-time workers rose form 27 to 37 percent among males and from 42 to 53 percent among females. Part-time workers accounted for 37 percent of all economically active males aged 70 to 74 in 1960 but for 50 percent in 1980; for working women of this age, the share working part-time rose from 48 to 62 percent. Finally, at ages 75 and over the share working part-time rose from 44 to 51 percent for men and from 47 to 59 percent for women. The increased eligi-bility for Social Security retirement, increases in the level of real benefits (relative to wages), and the existence of the earnings test have presumably interacted to produce this outcome.

In addition to age and gender, the labor force activity of older persons is also closely related to their educational attainment. A variety of symptomatic indicators of labor force activity in 1979 for males and females aged 55-59, 60-64, and 65 and over is shown in appendix 9. For several levels of educational attainment (less than elementary school, elementary school only, some secondary school, secondary school only, some college, and college degree), data are presented that show the share of the age-gender-education group that had any earnings in 1979, that usually worked thirty-five or more hours per week, and that worked forty or more weeks during the year. Generally, these measures would suggest increasing degrees of attachment to the labor force.

If we hold constant the effects of age and gender, these data permit consideration of the effects of educational attainment. With some minor exceptions (such as males aged 55-64 with seventeen or eighteen years of school or females aged 65 and over with sixteen years of school), the relationship between educational attainment and labor force activity is strongly monotonic and positive. Regardless of the measure of labor force activity chosen, persons with more education are increasingly more likely to be economically active than are others of the same age and gender. Furthermore, the relative importance of education to labor force participation increases with age within the limited age range for which data are available. For example, among males aged 55 to 59, the share of persons working forty or more weeks in 1979 was 81 percent for those with at least four years of college but only 69 percent for those with less education. This differential of about 18 percent increased to 30 percent among males aged 60 to 64 (65 and 50 percent) and to 112 percent among males over 65 (19 and 9 percent). The differential was much less pronounced among females but still increased from about 23 percent at ages 55 to 64 to 55 percent at ages 65 and above.

Persons who are currently employed are conventionally distributed into categories on the basis of either their occupation or the industry of their employer. Data that summarize both of these categorical distributions are presented in table 5.2. These data, which are for the years 1950 and 1980, reflect in large measure the changes in the structure of the U.S. economy over this period.

Table 5.2
Occupation and Industry of Employed Workers, United States,
1950 and 1980

(percent)

OCCUPATIONAL GROUP	1950 under 60	1950 over 60	1980 under 60	1980 over 60
Professional and Managerial	17.8%	19.4%	22.7%	22.0%
Clerical & Sales	20.2%	12.3%	30.5%	28.5%
Total White Collar	38.0%	31.7%	53.2%	50.5%
Blue Collar	41.0%	33.0%	31.6%	26.4%
Agricultural	11.2%	20.2%	2.6%	5.9%
Service	9.8%	14.4%	12.6%	17.2%
INDUSTRIAL GROUP				
Agriculture and Mining	13.5%	22.0%	3.8%	6.5%

Construction	6.2%	6.7%	6.0%	4.9%
Manufacturing	27.0%	20.0%	22.7%	19.2%
Transportation, Communications, Utilities	8.0%	6.7%	7.4%	5.5%
Trade	19.4%	15.7%	20.4%	20.3%
Finance and Business Services	6.0%	6.0%	10.2%	10.5%
Personal and Recreation Servcs	7.0%	9.6%	3.9%	7.4%
Professional Services	8.3%	9.3%	20.3%	20.7%
Public Administration	4.5%	4.0%	5.3%	5.0%

Source: 1950 and 1980 Censuses of Population

These changes, which suggest the transition from a manufacturing to a service base, are quite similar overall to those that have occurred in most industrialized societies. In terms of occupations, one might note that both younger and older workers were much more likely to be found in so-called white collar (that is, professional, managerial, sales and clerical occupations) and service occupations in 1980 than they were in 1950 and, conversely, less likely to be engaged in blue collar (that is, assembly, operative, and laborer occupations) or agricultural activities. Over time, older workers have been more likely than younger workers to be employed as service or agricultural workers, and relative differences by age have not changed much during the period, with the exception of the relative growth of older workers in lower-level white collar positions, which reflects the increases in labor force activity among older women. In terms of the industrial sector, there is relatively little difference in terms of differences over time between younger and older workers. Distributions by industry are quite similar for younger and older workers, and temporal changes are more or less parallel for the two age groups. There is the expected relative concentration of older workers in agriculture, but the share employed in this sector in 1980 was less than one-third the corresponding share in 1950.

The economic well-being of the older population is, of course, best measured by considering the levels of income that are available to this population. Income, in turn, may be measured for the individual or for the entire household in which an individual resides. Our discussion here will focus on both of these alternatives, beginning with income levels for individuals. Figure 5.1 illustrates trends in the level of income for persons aged 55 and over from 1950 to 1980 (data are not available separately for persons aged 60 and over in 1950 and 1960) as well as for persons aged 15 to 54. In 1980, median income for all persons aged 55 and over was about $7,700, or about 82 percent of the level observed among younger persons. During the thirty-year period under consideration here, median income among the elderly had risen by nearly 400 percent since 1950, an increase of about fifty percentage points more than that experienced by the younger population. Most of this differential is due to the favorable experience of older persons during the 1970s, when median income more than doubled as opposed to an increase of slightly more than 80 percent among

Figure 5.1
Mean Personal Income in Current and Constant (1980) Dollars,
by Age, 1950-1980

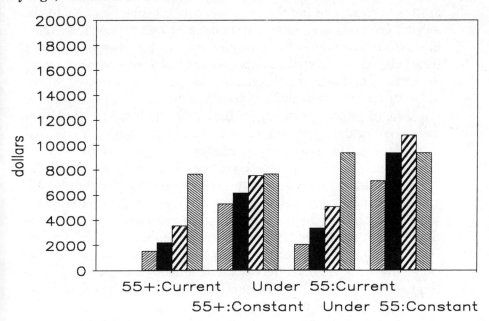

LEGEND

Source: U.S. Bureau of the Census, 1950-1980 Censuses of Population.

younger persons. During the first twenty years of the period, the median increased by a factor of 1.3 for those aged 55 + and by a factor of 1.4 for those aged 15 to 54 years.

In considering changes in levels of income over time, we must make adjustments for changes in prices or the purchasing power of the income that one receives. The discussion in the preceding paragraph has been in terms of unadjusted income, or income in so-called current dollars. However, because of sustained price increases throughout the entire period, these current dollar figures are not comparable for the purpose of measuring changes in the level of economic well-being. To make such comparisons, we must evaluate income levels by an index of relative prices, to assure something closer to strict comparability. These figures are termed "constant" dollar income levels; for our purposes, we have chosen to fix 1980 as the standard and to adjust incomes for prior years to the level of prices prevailing in that year. By comparing current and constant dollar income levels, one can see quite clearly that during the 1970s, the real purchasing power of younger Americans actually declined (to the level prevailing in 1960), while that for older Americans was nearly unchanged over the decade, but still substantially greater than that observed in 1960. The 1970s were a decade of high inflation unprecedented in the United States, and wage levels simply did not keep abreast of inflation. Older persons fared comparatively well during this decade because the level of Social Security retirement (and survivor) benefits rose in real (constant dollar) terms by some 25 percent, while real wages declined by about 3 percent.

A much more detailed perspective of the current picture of income levels among older individuals is afforded by table 5.3, which shows income and poverty rates in 1979 and 1987 for older persons according to age, gender, and race/ethnicity. Average income levels in the latter year range from a high of $26,642 among white males aged 60 to 64 to a low of $5,264 for black females aged 70 or over. Based on the more extensive census data for 1979, the following observed differentials in income are quite consistent:

1. for males, regardless of race, income at ages 75 and above is half that at ages 60 to 64;

2. for females, regardless of race, income at ages 75 and above is two-thirds to three-quarters that at ages 60 to 64;

Table 5.3
Mean Income by Age, Gender, and Race, United States, 1980 and 1987

1980	60-64	65-69	70-74	75+	75+ as % of 60-64
Male:					
Income					
Total	$17,459	$12,574	$10,451	$8,736	50%
White	$18,270	$13,197	$10,973	$9,156	50%
Black	$9,703	$6,747	$5,449	$4,582	47%
Hispanic	$11,548	$8,145	$6,423	$5,349	46%
Black as % of white	53%	51%	50%	50%	
Hispanic as % of white	63%	62%	59%	58%	
Poverty Rate					
Total	8	9	10	13	162%
White	7	7	9	12	171%
Black	22	25	29	34	155%
Hispanic	17	19	23	25	147%
Black as % of white	314%	357%	322%	283%	
Hispanic as % of white	243%	271%	256%	208%	

Table 5.3 (continued)

1980	60-64	65-69	70-74	75+	75+ as % of 60-64
Female:					
Total	$7,124	$5,828	$5,691	$5,366	75%
White	$7,346	$6,035	$5,909	$5,557	76%
Black	$5,297	$4,080	$3,635	$3,271	62%
Hispanic	$5,076	$3,960	$3,613	$3,557	70%
Black as % of white	72%	68%	62%	59%	
Hispanic as % of white	69%	66%	61%	64%	
Poverty Rate					
Total	12	13	16	22	183%
White	10	11	14	20	200%
Black	32	35	40	43	134%
Hispanic	24	26	29	30	125%
Black as % of white	320%	318%	286%	215%	
Hispanic as % of white	240%	236%	207%	150%	
Female as % of Male:					
Income: 1980					
Total	41%	46%	54%	61%	
White	40%	46%	54%	61%	
Black	55%	60%	67%	71%	
Hispanic	44%	49%	56%	66%	

Poverty:1980

Total	150%	144%	160%	169%
White	143%	157%	156%	167%
Black	145%	140%	138%	126%
Hispanic	141%	137%	126%	120%

1987

Male:

Income	60-64	65-69	70+
Total	$25,531	$18,821	$15,042
White	$26,642	$19,598	$15,666
Black	$14,517	$10,526	$8,412
Black as % of white	54%	54%	54%

Poverty Rate	60-64	65+
Total	10	9
White	8	7
Black	27	25
Hispanic	14	23
Black as % of white	341%	362%
Hispanic % of white	179%	344%

1987

Female:

	60-64	65-69	70+
Total	$10,570	$9,768	$9,443
White	$10,911	$10,184	$9,896
Black	$8,279	$6,024	$5,264
Black as % of white	77%	59%	53%

111

Table 5.3 (continued)

1987	60-64	65+	
Poverty Rate			
Total	12	15	
White	10	13	
Black	32	40	
Hispanic	27	31	
Black as % of white	328%	322%	
Hispanic % of white	280%	244%	
Female as % of Male			
Income: 1987			
Total	41%	52%	63%
White	41%	52%	63%
Black	57%	57%	63%
Poverty:1987			
Total	124%	175%	
White	124%	184%	
Black	120%	163%	
Hispanic	194%	130%	

Sources: 1980 Census of Population
US Bureau of the Census, 1989a, p. 132-136
US Bureau of the Census, 1989b, p. 29-31

3. for males, regardless of age, income among blacks is about half that of whites, and income among Hispanics is about three-fifths that of whites;

4. for females, regardless of age, income among blacks and Hispanics is about two-thirds that of whites;

5. among white and Hispanic females under age 70, income is about half that of males; this increases with age so that at ages 75 and above the fraction approaches two-thirds; and, finally,

6. among black females, income is half to three-fourths of the level prevailing among males of the same age; the female-to-male ratio also steadily rises with age.

Table 5.3 also provides data on the relative incidence of poverty; this is a concept defined by the U.S. Office of Management and Budget that relates actual income to that level needed for minimum standards of housing, nutrition, and other necessities. In 1987, the poverty level for a person aged 65 or more years living alone was $5,447; that for a two-person household headed by an older person was $6,872. As would be expected from the previous discussion, poverty rates are lower among males than among females, are lower among whites than among persons of other races, and are lower among the younger elderly than among the older elderly. The interaction of some of these variables is illustrated in figure 5.2, which indicates how these and other variables produce a range of poverty incidence that even exceeds the 7-43 percent range shown in table 5.3.

The other perspective on income, namely that at the household level, is provided by the data in table 5.4, which also is limited to a detailed portrayal of current income differentials according to demographic charactristics of the householder. It should be recognized that these data will pertain not to all older persons in the United States, but rather only to those who reside in a household headed by a person at least 60 or 65 years of age. Hence, those individuals who live with a relative or other person under age 60 who is the householder are excluded from this analysis— here, the focus is solely upon "older households." It might be noted in passing that the economic well-being of the elderly who reside with younger relatives is often superior, on the household level, to that of the elderly who maintain their own household, because of the higher income levels of younger persons (Serow, 1982). Once again, it is quite apparent that differences in demographic char-

Figure 5.2
Percent of Elderly below the Poverty Level by Selected Characteristics, 1986

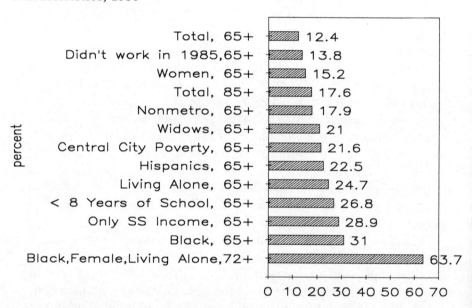

Source: U.S. Bureau of the Census, 1989b, pp. 7-135.

Table 5.4
Mean Household Income by Age, Gender, and Race of Head,
United States, 1980 and 1987

1980	Total	White	Black	Hispanic
Head aged				
60 to 64:				
Male Head of household	$24,155	$24,964	$16,202	$18,334
married couple	$25,199	$25,733	$18,146	$19,628
wife in labor force	$28,376	$28,890	$22,295	$24,155
wife not in labor force	$23,364	$23,959	$14,866	$17,109
other male head	$21,177	$22,720	$14,698	$17,462
unrelated individual	$12,025	$13,159	$7,141	$8,076
living alone	$12,610	$13,632	$7,486	$8,265
Female Head of household	$16,255	$17,694	$11,823	$12,575
in labor force	$19,334	$20,503	$15,018	$16,304
not in labor force	$13,613	$15,097	$9,552	$10,487
unrelated individual	$8,719	$9,207	$5,219	$5,344
living alone	$8,900	$9,360	$5,302	$5,520

Table 5.4 (continued)

1980
Head aged 65+:

	Total	White	Black	Hispanic
Male Head of household	$16,831	$17,369	$11,350	$12,813
married couple	$17,092	$17,480	$11,764	$13,153
wife in labor force	$22,393	$22,969	$16,903	$19,133
wife not in labor force	$16,093	$16,498	$10,236	$11,779
other male head	$17,379	$18,567	$11,976	$13,347
unrelated individual	$8,418	$9,048	$4,829	$5,563
living alone	$8,601	$9,176	$4,903	$5,655
Female Head of household	$15,145	$16,295	$10,342	$11,387
in labor force	$18,698	$20,239	$13,190	$15,750
not in labor force	$14,714	$15,835	$9,928	$10,927
unrelated individual	$6,784	$7,067	$3,946	$4,324
living alone	$6,817	$7,087	$3,855	$4,412

Relative to White Male

Head aged 60 to 54:

	Black Male	Hispanic Male	White Female	Black Female	Hispanic Female
Male Head of household	65%	73%	71%	47%	50%
married couple	71%	76%			
female in labor force	77%	84%	71%	52%	56%
female not in labor force	62%	71%	63%	40%	44%
other male head	65%	77%			
unrelated individual	54%	61%	70%	40%	41%
living alone	55%	61%	69%	39%	40%

116

Head aged
65+:

	Total	White	Black		
Male Head of household	65%	74%	94%	60%	66%
married couple	67%	75%	88%	57%	69%
female in labor force	74%	83%	96%	60%	66%
female not in labor force	62%	71%			
other male head	65%	72%			
unrelated individual	53%	61%	78%	43%	48%
living alone	53%	62%	77%	42%	48%

1987
Head aged
65+:

	Total	White	Black	Black % of white
Total	$19,933	$20,647	$12,334	60%
Unrelated individuals	$11,909	$12,476	$6,690	54%
male	$14,415	$15,468	$7,162	46%
female	$11,156	$11,622	$6,457	56%
Total families	$27,107	$27,895	$17,800	64%
married couple	$27,489	$28,035	$18,061	64%
wife in labor force	$37,566	$38,674	$26,104	67%
wife not in labor force	$25,820	$26,418	$15,725	60%
other male head	$29,101	$30,031	NA	NA
other female head	$24,350	$26,380	$16,156	61%

Sources: 1980 Census of Population
         U.S. Bureau of the Census, 1989e, p. 28

acteristics of the householder lead to profound differences in levels of household income. Mean household income in 1979 ranged from nearly $30,000 for households headed by a married white male aged 60 to 64 where the wife was (also) in the labor force to slightly less than $4,000 for a black female aged 65 or more living alone. Similarly, in 1987, the range between these extremes was nearly $39,000 to $6,500. Once again, quite consistent differences in household income levels emerge, depending upon the age, race, and gender of the householder. With the exception of persons living alone, households headed by black or Hispanic males receive about two-thirds and three-fourths, respectively, of the income of identically configured households headed by white males, regardless of the age of the householder. In the case of persons living alone, these fractions are reduced to about half and three-fifths, respectively. Among female-headed households, the age of the householder plays some role in the size of the income differential: differences are somewhat greater for those households where the head is aged 60 to 64, presumably reflecting the higher level of labor force participation and earnings among males at this age.

Many of these differences in levels of income will be reflected in the sources of income that are available to older households. Table 5.5 presents summary data for 1980 that show the sources of income depending upon household type, that is, for family households (two or more persons related by blood or marriage) or for persons living alone. The data are also classified by the poverty status of the household, thus affording some opportunity to consider the role of income differences. Wages and earnings account for a much larger share of income among higher income households, regardless of type (30 and 4 percent of total income, respectively) and a much larger share of income for families than for single individuals, regardless of level of income (35 and 13 percent, respectively). Social Security and public assistance account for 90 percent of the income of the elderly poor, but only one-third of the income among the nonpoor. Conversely, income from assets and other sources (primarily privately funded pensions) provide nearly 40 percent of the income of the nonpoor elderly, but less than 10 percent of that accruing to the poor. A recent study by Burkhauser, Holden, and Feaster (1988) points out the dramatic role that pension income and marital status play in the determination of poverty among the elderly. The dissolution of a marriage greatly increases the risk of poverty for the widow, and this risk is magnified considerably if the husband was either without a private pension or if the pension terminated with his death. It must be noted in this regard, though, that the economic circumstances of the poor are somewhat mitigated by the existence of "in-kind" benefits (subsidized medical care, food, and housing) that are not included in the calculation of income and, therefore, that are not included in the determination of poverty status. One study by Smeeding (1982) suggested that the complete valuation of all in-kind benefits could reduce reported poverty levels among the elderly (based solely upon money income) by as much as two-thirds.

It has recently become possible to obtain data on the wealth of the population of the United States. Wealth is defined here as net worth, which is the difference between gross assets (financial assets and property equity) and liabilities. In 1984, median wealth of all American families was slightly less than $33,000. Among all families with head aged 55 and over, median wealth was some $66,000. Even among families whose head was aged 75 or over, median wealth ($55,000) was some 70 percent higher than the average for all families, while for those families with head aged 55 to 74 years median wealth was approximately $70,000. While older families accounted for some 36 percent of all families, these same families held nearly twice this share of the nation's wealth (U.S. Bureau of the Census, 1986). Unfortunately, such data, now collected in the Survey of Income and Program Participation, have not been collected with any regularity in the past, so there exists no basis for discussing past trends in the concentration of wealth as a function of the age of family heads.

The final aspect of income and economic well-being to be addressed is the disposition of income, or patterns of consumer expenditures among older households. These data, which are for the year 1985, are summarized in table 5.6. Although total expenditures among older households are, on average, less than those of younger households, a large portion of the difference is the result of the smaller size of the typical older household. Levels of per capita consumption among older households are about the same (or greater) than those reported for younger households, except among households where the head is 75 or more years of age. The elderly generally spend slightly more of their budget on necessities such as food and housing and somewhat less on transporta-

Table 5.5
Sources of Income for Older Households, United States, 1980

(percent distribution)

All Households	Total	Non-Poor	Poor
Wages and earnings	25%	30%	4%
wages	21%	25%	4%
self-employment	4%	5%	-0%
Other	75%	70%	96%
social security	39%	31%	75%
public assistance	4%	2%	14%
assets	20%	24%	3%
other	12%	14%	4%
Families			
Wages and earnings	35%	38%	10%
wages	29%	32%	11%
self-employment	6%	6%	-1%

Other	65%	62%	90%
social security	31%	27%	69%
public assistance	2%	1%	14%
assets	19%	20%	2%
other	13%	13%	5%
Unrelated Individuals			
Wages and earnings	13%	17%	2%
wages	11%	14%	2%
self-employment	2%	3%	-0%
Other	97%	83%	98%
social security	48%	36%	77%
public assistance	5%	2%	14%
assets	22%	30%	4%
other	12%	15%	4%

Source: 1980 Census of Population

Table 5.6
Expenditure Patterns by Age of Householder, United States, 1985

	Total	Head <55	Head 55-64	Head 65+	Head 65-74	Head 75+
(percent of total expenditures)						
Total expenditures	$22,217	$24,156	$23,390	$15,167	$17,000	$12,347
Mean Household Size	2.6	2.9	2.4	1.8	2.0	1.6
Per Capita expenditures	$8,545	$8,330	$9,746	$8,232	$8,500	$7,717
Food	15.3%	14.9%	15.6%	16.9%	17.2%	16.4%
Alcohol	1.3%	1.4%	1.1%	.9%	1.1%	.7%
Housing	30.1%	30.5%	26.8%	31.8%	30.6%	33.7%
Apparel	5.2%	5.5%	5.0%	3.8%	4.4%	2.9%
Transportation	20.5%	21.1%	20.6%	17.1%	18.9%	14.3%
Health	4.7%	3.4%	5.5%	10.3%	9.1%	12.2%
Entertainment	4.9%	5.3%	4.4%	3.4%	3.9%	2.6%
Personal Care	.9%	.8%	1.0%	1.2%	1.2%	1.2%
Reading	.6%	.6%	.7%	.8%	.8%	.8%
Education	1.4%	1.7%	.9%	.4%	.5%	.2%
Tobacco	1.0%	1.0%	1.0%	.8%	1.0%	.6%
Contributions	3.6%	2.6%	5.1%	7.2%	4.9%	10.7%
Insurance and pension	9.1%	9.7%	10.6%	3.8%	4.9%	2.1%
Miscellaneous	1.5%	1.4%	1.8%	1.6%	1.7%	1.5%

Source: US Bureau of Labor Statistics, 1987

tion than do younger households. The effect of these differences is largely offsetting, so that two-thirds of the expenditures of all consumer units are dedicated to these three primary consumption groups. The most striking difference is in the area of health care, where households with head age 65 + spend three times the share of income that households with a head under the age of 55 spend. This difference persists despite the Medicare program, which is, in essence, a national health insurance program that exists solely for persons aged at least 65 years. Offsetting the difference in health care expenditures is the much lower proportion of consumption by older households that is expended upon insurance premiums and savings for private pensions.

The final aspect of the socioeconomic characteristics of the older population that will be considered in this book is their educational attainment. Table 5.7 summarizes the median level of years of school completed among all persons aged 20 and over (by five-year age intervals through age 75 and over) from 1940 to 1980. The data are arranged so that one can consider differences in educational attainment by age, by period, and by cohort. The table can be read in three ways:

1. by row (horizontally), showing median educational attainment for a stated birth cohort over time; generally, there will be little change as the cohort ages except for that attributable to differential mortality;
2. by column (vertically), showing median educational attainment for successive cohorts in a given age group; for any given age, the uppermost figures in each column represent the current (1980) cohort in that age group; and
3. diagonally, showing the age structure of educational attainment for each of the five periods in question.

Age, period, and cohort effects all interact to produce noticeable changes in the levels of educational attainment among the older population. In each of the three census years from 1940 through 1960, members of the older population had completed, on average, incrementally more than eight years of school, regardless of current age. Because of successively higher levels of completed schooling among younger elements of the population, the older population became increasingly distanced from the remainder of the population. In 1970 and particularly in 1980, this situation began to change as the cohorts that aged into the ranks of those 60

Table 5.7
Educational Attainment by Age, 1940-1980 (median years of school)

birth Period	current age											
	20-24	25-29	30-34	35-39	40-44	45-49	50-54	55-59	60-64	65-69	70-74	75+
1955-1959	12.3											
1950-1955		12.9										
1945-1950	12.7		12.9									
1940-1945		12.5		12.7								
1935-1940	12.3		12.4		12.6							
1930-1935		12.3		12.3		12.5						

124

1925–1930	12.1	12.2	12.3	12.4	
1920–1925	12.1	12.1	12.2	12.3	
1915–1920	11.2	11.9	11.8	12.1	12.1
1910–1915	10.3	10.5	10.6	10.9	11.0
1905–1910	9.5	9.8	9.7	10.0	10.1
1900–1905	8.8	8.9	8.8	9.0	9.4 (1980)
1895–1900	8.6	8.7	8.6	8.7	
1890–1895	8.5	8.5	8.4	8.4	8.5 (1970)
1885–1890	8.4	8.4	8.3		

Table 5.7 (continued)

	current age											
birth Period	20-24	25-29	30-34	35-39	40-44	45-49	50-54	55-59	60-64	65-69	70-74	75+
1880-1885								8.3		9.2		9.2 (1960)
1875-1880									8.3		8.2	
1870-1875										8.2		8.1 (1950)
1865-1870												8.0
before 1865											8.1	(1940)

Source: 1940-1990 Censuses of Population

or more years old were appreciably better educated. In 1980, persons who were 60 to 64 years of age had, on average, 1.1 to 2.7 more years of school than did all older cohorts, but a maximum of only 0.8 years fewer than any younger cohort. By way of contrast, as recently as 1960, the median education level of those aged 60-64 exceeded that of all older cohorts by a maximum of only 0.4 years but trailed behind younger cohorts by as much as 3.7 years. It is also clear from the uppermost diagonal of table 5.7 that future generations of the older population will hardly differ from younger elements of the population in terms of educational attainment. This higher degree of education will undoubtedly have some considerable impact on the tastes and expectations of future generations of older Americans and should provide them with comparatively high levels of retirement income if present patterns of association between earnings and educational attainment persist into the future.

6

HEALTH STATUS OF THE OLDER POPULATION

With the dramatic increase in the number of persons aged 60 and older, their health status and their demand for health resources become a critical component of a country's aging population. This chapter will deal with four aspects of the health status of the older population: morbidity, disability, health expectancy, and causes of death. Related to these aspects of an aging population, data will be presented on patterns of health care utilization and costs. Unlike most of the data presented thus far, which are largely census-based, the source of the data to be analyzed here is from the U.S. National Center for Health Statistics' National Health Interview Survey, Multiple Cause-of-Death Public Use files and other periodic surveys conducted by this agency. Because these are comparatively recent activities, it will largely be impossible to present any data that are suggestive of trends in these aspects of the health status of the older population, with the exception of multiple cause-of-death data, which date back to 1968.

Current summary data on the prevalence of selected chronic conditions in the older population by age, gender, race, and income are shown in table 6.1. Arthritis is the most prevalent condition in the older population, followed by hypertension, hearing impairments, deformity, cataracts, and ischemic heart disease. This ranking holds for each specific age group, with the exception of cataracts, which become the fourth prevalent condition in the

Table 6.1
Chronic Conditions Reported by Older Persons, by Age, Gender, and Race,
United States, 1982-1984

(per 1000 persons)

	Cataracts	Other Visual	Hearing	Defor- mity	Ischemic Heart Disease	Hyper- tension	Cerebro- vascular	Emphy- sema	Chronic Bron- chitis	Diabetes	Arth- ritis
55 to 64											
Total	31	56	181	150	93	307	23	32	51	72	351
W.Male	27	72	255	151	142	286	25	51	42	64	280
B.Male	21	80	75	186	60	365	48	23	46	153	293
W.Female	33	36	129	145	60	301	17	16	56	63	413
B.Female	34	98	152	169	38	504	30	27	79	149	471
65+											
Total	149	98	309	168	136	395	58	41	58	91	496
W.Male	105	106	368	144	178	317	63	75	53	80	392
B.Male	80	148	262	171	61	371	108	41	16	121	468
W.Female	186	89	276	180	119	429	50	20	67	85	540
B.Female	136	113	261	265	77	643	76	12	36	211	640
65 to 74											
Total	94	73	261	165	137	394	42	43	63	94	476
W.Male	64	84	329	146	192	335	53	74	52	74	391
W.Female	121	62	220	175	110	414	30	24	75	90	527

130

75 to 84											
Total	218	120	361	162	135	398	81	41	51	87	498
W.Male	164	128	430	133	148	289	80	85	57	92	386
W.Female	259	109	320	176	138	446	75	18	55	80	560
85+											
Total	327	219	496	211	122	393	100	17	43	81	520
W.Male	283	247	508	168	168	245	95	40	33	86	439
W.Female	355	198	493	224	108	464	100	3	53	70	556
By Income:											
65 to 74											
<$10,000	125	76	273	227	125	490	66	58	75	97	574
$10-19,999	106	80	273	143	140	391	61	25	61	100	431
$20-34,999	34	79	272	106	96	345	20	63	71	94	358
$35,000+	42	50	197	126	146	421	52	56	68	50	209
75+											
<$10,000	260	133	404	201	155	464	92	33	58	123	562
$10-19,999	255	144	374	236	126	405	114	57	83	89	513
$20-34,999	240	193	444	162	274	419	87	26	15	98	348
$35,000+	229	169	532	192	200	428	186	NA	63	174	434

Source: US National Center for Health Statistics, 1987b, p. 23-24

131

population 75 and older. For most conditions shown, prevalence rates rise with age, particularly for cataracts and other visual impairments, for hearing impairments, for arthritis, and for cerebrovascular disease. For several other conditions, most notably ischemic heart disease, hypertension, and diabetes, prevalence increases markedly between ages 55-64 and 65-74, but changes very little thereafter. One must bear in mind that among those aged 75 and over, and especially among those 85 and over, a certain amount of natural selectivity is already present in the population and that those who survived to these ages in fact did so because they were comparatively healthy in the first place.

There are some important differentials by gender and race. Among whites, males are more likely to have ischemic heart disease, cerebrovascular disease (except for 85+), and emphysema than are females, but less likely to have chronic bronchitis (except for 65-74) and arthritis. Blacks are more likely to have hypertension, cerebrovascular disease, and diabetes than whites but are less likely to have ischemic heart disease. It is interesting to note that males are more prone to conditions that lead to sudden mortality, while females tend to have conditions leading to prolonged morbidity. The role of income with respect to the prevalence of these conditions is rarely clear-cut. Higher incomes are associated with a lower prevalence of cataracts, orthopedic deformities, and arthritis.

An additional perspective on the prevalence of chronic conditions can be obtained by examining hospital discharge rates as shown in table 6.2. One caution, however, in examining these data is that they are not corrected for multiple discharges in a given year. Discharge rates usually increase with age, with the exception of neoplasms in females 85+. Rates are nearly always higher in males than females. Given that the data are available for only two points in time, one may observe upward trends for discharges for circulatory conditions regardless of age and gender, except for females 85+. Rates are relatively stable for stroke and neoplasms except among males 75+. Data on hospital discharges reflect levels of both the prevalence of conditions as well as the utilization of health care facilities.

One of the more crucial aspects of the health status of the older population is the degree to which chronic morbidity and other health problems impose some disability and limitation on the activities of daily living. Disability greatly increases with age as can be

Table 6.2
Discharges from Short-Stay Hospitals, by Age, Gender, and Primary Diagnosis,
United States, 1979 and 1984

(per 1000) persons

	Cerebrovascular		Neoplasms		Hypertension		Fractures		Heart	
	1979	1984	1979	1984	1979	1984	1979	1984	1979	1984
MALE:										
55-64	6	7	19	20	6	6			42	47
65-74	16	17	41	41	15	15			61	72
75-84	34	39	54	58	19	22			97	98
85+	47	64	55	63	17	10			127	141
FEMALE:										
55-64	5	5	20	24			6	5	23	25
65-74	12	13	27	30			11	11	43	50
75-84	30	29	31	37			25	23	79	92
85+	46	46	28	26			52	50	109	102

Source: US National Center for Health Statistics, 1987b, p. 64-65

seen in figure 6.1. The proportion of the civilian noninstitutional population that has some form of limitation in the activities of daily living goes from 7 percent in the age group 65-74 to 16 percent in the age group 75-84 and 44 percent in the oldest old age group. These proportions, while still increasing with age, also vary by race and gender as can be observed in figure 6.2. Black females have a larger proportion of their population limited in their activities than any other demographic group. Although blacks are more likely to be limited in their activities than whites, this differential is decreasing with age. Among whites, males tend to be equally likely as females to be limited in their daily activities, but among blacks, females are slightly more likely than males to have activity limitations.

The specific types of activities that older persons have difficulty in accomplishing are presented in table 6.3. Among the non-institutionalized population, the share of persons with specified limitations in the activities of daily living increases with age. Not only are males less likely to experience each type of activity limitation at each age than are females, but the rate of increase in activity limitation with advancing age among males is appreciably less than among females. Having difficulty in walking is the most predominant form of activity limitation, involving more than 10 percent of the population in each age group for both males and females. Other limitations in daily activities are observed in less than 10 percent of the population until the oldest age groups (i.e., 85+ for males and 75+ for females).

As one can see in table 6.4, activity limitations among residents of nursing homes are more common and more limiting than those reported by the noninstitutionalized population. Limitations on such elementary activities as eating and dressing, which occur less than one time in five even among the oldest members of the noninstitutionalized population, are quite common, as are problems of continence and walking. It is, of course, the presence of limitations such as these, often complicated by the presence of mental impairments such as Alzheimer's disease and other chronic conditions, that impels the older individuals or their families to seek institutionalization in the first place.

In the previous sections we have observed increases in both morbidity and disability among the older population. With the increase in life expectancy that has occurred in the United States, the question to examine is whether or not the health status of the elderly

Figure 6.1
Percent of Civilian Noninstitutionalized Population with Severe
Limitation of Activities of Daily Living, by Age, 1979

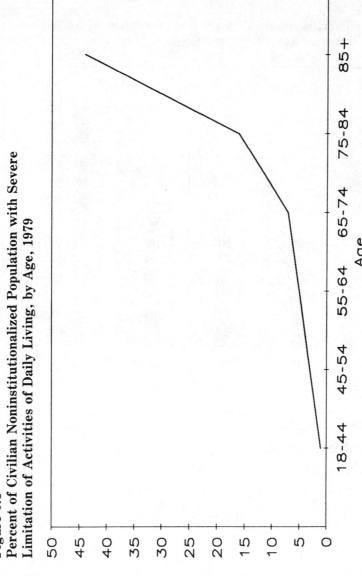

Source: U.S. National Center for Health Statistics, 1987b, *Health Statistics on Older Persons, 1986*, pp. 2, 33.

Figure 6.2
Percent of Persons Aged 55+ with Any Limitation of Activities
of Daily Living, by Age, Race, and Gender, 1984

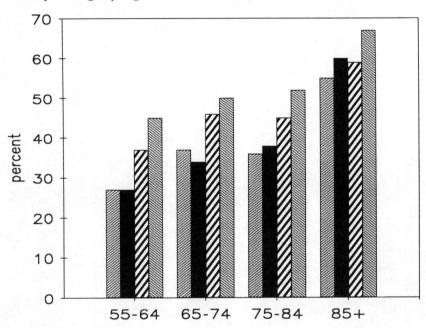

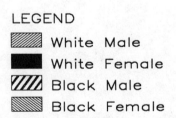

LEGEND
White Male
White Female
Black Male
Black Female

Source: U.S. National Center for Health Statistics, 1987b.

Table 6.3
Percentage of Older Population with Specified Limitations in the
Activities of Daily Living, by Age and Gender, United States, 1985

(non-institutional population)

	Male				Female			
	55-64	65-74	75-84	85+	55-64	65-74	75-84	85+
walking:								
up 10 stairs	9	13	18	32	10	15	26	43
1/4 mile	12	16	22	37	16	23	33	51
lifting								
10 lbs	16	22	29	48	16	25	39	62
going out	5	7	10	20	9	13	24	41
getting	3	5	8	22	4	7	15	35
out of bed	4	5	6	13	6	7	11	22
bathing	4	6	9	23	5	7	14	30
eating	1	2	3	4	1	1	2	4
dressing	4	4	7	14	3	4	8	18

Source: US National Center for Health Statistics, 1987b, p. 45-55

Table 6.4
Percentage of Nursing Home Residents with Specified Limitations
in the Activities of Daily Living, by Age and Gender, United States,
1985

	Male				Female			
	55-64	65-74	75-84	85+	55-64	65-74	75-84	85+
Dressing	60	64	71	77	65	74	78	83
Toilet Use	41	49	55	62	52	61	62	70
Walking	48	55	65	78	55	64	71	83
Continence	31	39	54	58	36	45	55	58
Eating	29	33	32	39	31	34	42	45
Vision	12	14	25	29	11	19	21	67
Hearing	8	9	22	38	4	10	15	67

Source: US National Center for Health Statistics, 1987b, p. 75

has improved. Table 6.5 shows the total number of years a person is expected to live and how many of these years will be in good health. These data appear to show that increasing life expectancy may not be accompanied by corresponding improvements in healthy life without activity restriction. For example, males in 1976 were expected to live 68.7 years, but 11.5 of those years have some restriction of activity associated with them. Females have experienced an increase of 3.3 years in life expectancy between 1962 and 1976 (72.5 to 75.8), but only 2 of those years gained are expected to be spent in good health. Both males and females are expected to have 1.5 more years lived with some restriction of activity in 1976 than they did in 1962.

A model is depicted in figure 6.3 describing the change in the proportion of a cohort (U.S. females, 1980) that can expect to survive to a given age without one of three basic types of health events occurring—morbidity, disability, or mortality. In figure 6.3 the horizontal axis represents age and the vertical axis describes the probability (expressed as a percent) of surviving to a given age without suffering one of the health events. The spatial relation of the three curves can be used to interpolate changes in the health burden of society of age-related morbidity and disability. Specifically, the areas in the figure are defined by a product of age (time) and the average probability (that is, the frequency within a population of being ill or disabled). Consequently, the areas describe the number of person years that the cohort or life table population occupies specific health states. Area A represents the number of person years spent free of disease, area B represents the number of years spent with chronic disease but unimpaired, and area C represents the number of person years a given cohort can expect to be disabled. Areas A + B combined represent productive life expectancy (Manton and Soldo, 1985). The purpose of presenting this model is that it can be used to describe the health status of the older population at a given time as well as to forecast changes in the health status over time. For example, the complex interrelationships of morbidity, disability, and mortality can be untangled within such a model. We can show how each of these areas will increase or decrease as a response to health trends and preventative programs.

Data on cause-of-death trends are a useful indicator of the health status of the older population. There are actually two types of cause-specific mortality data that could be examined. The first

Table 6.5
Life Expectancy at Birth and Mean Health Expectancy in Various
States, by Gender, United States, 1962-1976

	1962	1969	1976	Change
MALES				
Life expectancy at birth	66.8	66.6	68.7	1.9
In good health	56.8	57.0	57.1	0.3
With activity restriction	10.0	9.7	11.5	1.5
FEMALES				
Life expectancy at birth	72.5	74.2	75.8	3.3
In good health	60.8	63.6	62.7	1.9
With activity restriction	11.6	10.6	13.1	1.5

Sources: US National Center for Health Statistics, 1988
National Health Interview Survey (unpublished date from tape files)

Figure 6.3
The Mortality (Observed), Morbidity (Hypothetical), and Disability
(Hypothetical) Survival Curves for U.S. Females in 1980

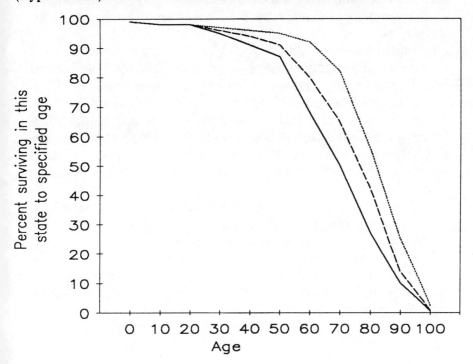

LEGEND

_____ Morbidity

___. Disability

.... Mortality

Source: Adapted from Manton and Soldo, 1985, p. 210.

is underlying cause-of-death data as presented in chapter 2 (tables
2.6 and 2.7). Such data do not fully describe the set of medical conditions identified at death. Data that contain all conditions listed
on the death certificate are called "multiple cause" mortality data
and are viewed as providing a more accurate depiction of mortality at advanced ages (see Manton and Stallard, 1984). These data
were obtained from the National Center for Health Statistics,
Multiple-Cause-of-Death Public Use files, 1968-1982, and tabula-
tions were done at the Center for Demographic Studies at Duke
University.

Multiple cause mortality of the older population is a significant
component of a country's aging population. The oldest old are the
fastest growing population and are expected to consume the largest amount of federal benefits; that is, by 2000 it is projected that,
under current federal policy, this population will consume $85.5
billion (in 1984 dollars) of benefits (Torrey, 1985). A significant
proportion of these benefits will be for the treatment of medical
conditions during the last years of life (Rabin, 1985). Multiple
cause-of-death data, therefore, not only will provide a good measure of mortality trends in the older population but also will be
useful for forecasting need for health care services and projections
of the costs in treating these conditions.

The count of the number of causes associated with death in the
older population describes the complexity of the disease process.
In the United States there is an average of 2.5 causes per death
for the total population. For those over 65, the average number of
causes per death is 2.8 for whites and 2.6 for nonwhites. The number of causes of death is also higher for chronic degenerative
diseases.

In table 6.6 trends in age-specific mortality rates for six leading
causes of death among the older population are shown. These
causes represent over 80 percent of all deaths, and because the
trends follow a monotonic pattern, we present data only for 1968,
1973, 1978, and 1982. Two different types of mortality rates are
presented as well as the ratio of the two rates. The underlying
cause (UC) rate is the traditional measure of mortality and is
based on a single cause of death. The total mention (TM) rate is the
multiple cause measure of mortality and is based on the total
number of times a cause is mentioned on the death certificate. The
ratio of the TM to UC rates represents the likelihood that a given
cause will be coded as a nonunderlying cause of death. Causes

Table 6.6
Age-specific Mortality Rates per 100,000 for Selected Causes of Death, by Underlying Cause (UC), and Total Mentions (TM), United States, 1968-1982

	65-74			75-84			85+		
	UC	TM	Ratio	UC	TM	Ratio	UC	TM	Ratio
HEART DISEASE									
1968	1,635	2,060	1.26	3,744	4,734	1.26	8,399	10,413	1.24
1973	1,478	1,940	1.31	3,379	4,454	1.32	8,185	10,524	1.29
1978	1,254	1,736	1.38	2,951	4,082	1.38	7,385	9,917	1.34
1982	1,187	1,751	1.47	2,803	4,069	1.45	7,324	10,257	1.40
% Change									
1968-82	-27.4%	-15.0%	17.0%	-25.2%	-14.1%	14.8%	-12.8%	-1.5%	13.0%
CANCER									
1968	750	851	1.13	1,110	1,361	1.23	1,335	1,804	1.35
1973	776	981	1.14	1,112	1,370	1.23	1,402	1,919	1.37
1978	815	919	1.13	1,196	1,453	1.21	1,512	2,053	1.36
1982	846	953	1.13	1,238	1,489	1.20	1,597	2,143	1.34
% Change									
1968-82	12.8%	12.0%	-.7%	11.5%	9.4%	-1.9%	19.6%	18.8%	-.7%

Table 6.6 (continued)

	65-74			75-84			85+		
	UC	TM	Ratio	UC	TM	Ratio	UC	TM	Ratio
CEREBROVASCULAR									
1968	410	652	1.59	1,290	1,981	1.54	3,264	4,689	1.44
1973	359	583	1.62	1,154	1,818	1.58	3,123	4,678	1.50
1978	248	423	1.71	841	1,389	1.65	2,379	3,761	1.58
1982	197	346	1.76	674	1,144	1.70	2,000	3,257	1.63
% Change 1968-82	-52.0%	-46.9%	10.4%	-47.8%	-42.3%	10.5%	-38.7%	-30.5%	13.4%
INFLUENZA/PNEUMONIA									
1968	106	387	3.65	324	1,079	3.33	1,057	2,977	2.82
1973	93	321	3.87	277	940	3.39	889	2,621	2.95
1978	67	259	3.87	242	772	3.19	875	2,329	2.66
1982	48	190	3.96	183	571	3.12	744	1,885	2.53
% Change 1968-82	-54.7%	-50.9%	8.4%	-43.5%	-47.1%	-6.3%	-29.6%	-36.7%	-10.0%

144

DIABETES

1968	96	344	3.58	184	665	3.61	233	843	3.62
1973	96	340	3.95	168	678	4.04	240	974	4.06
1978	66	268	4.06	135	557	4.13	221	873	3.95
1982	62	260	4.19	126	526	4.17	211	850	4.03
% Change 1968-82	-35.4%	-24.4%	17.0%	-31.5%	-20.9%	15.5%	-9.4%	.8%	11.3%

CHRONIC OBSTRUCTIVE RESPIRATORY DISEASE

1968	95	229	2.41	136	381	2.80	140	462	3.30
1973	111	268	2.41	165	448	2.72	177	554	3.13
1978	124	285	2.30	203	506	2.49	231	647	2.80
1982	134	310	2.31	237	567	2.39	273	747	2.74
% Change 1968-82	41.1%	35.4%	-4.0%	74.3%	48.8%	-14.6%	95.0%	61.7%	-17.1%

Source: National Center for Health Statistics, Multiple Cause of Death Public Use Tapes

145

such as influenza/pneumonia, diabetes, and chronic obstructive respiratory disease all have ratios above 2, indicating that these diseases are at least twice as likely to be coded as a nonunderlying cause of death. One can observe the downward trends in mortality because of heart disease and stroke or cerebrovascular disease. However, the rate of decline is much slower when the TM rates are examined. A good example of this difference is seen for heart disease among the oldest old (i.e., 85 +). When the traditional measure of mortality is used, there is a 12.8 percent decrease in mortality. When the TM rate is examined, the rate of decline is negligible at 1.5 percent. Cancer mortality increased at a similar rate for both UC and TM desginations. Influenza and pneumonia have declined over the fifteen-year period, but the rate of decline is much more rapid when the total mention of the disease is examined in the population 75 years and older. This effect is also observed by noting the decrease in the TM/UC ratio in the oldest age groups. Thus, influenza and pneumonia appear to be becoming more important as an underlying cause of death in the older population. Diabetes is much more likely to be a nonunderlying cause of death, as seen from the large TM/UC ratios. One observes a slower rate of decline in diabetes mortality when TM rates are analyzed. In fact, in the oldest old age group, there is a relatively constant rate for the total mention of diabetes (0.8 percent increase). Chronic obstructive respiratory disease has the largest rate of increase of any of the causes, although the change is slower when total mentions are examined. There is also a decline in the likelihood that this disease will be a nonunderlying cause.

The ranking of the relative frequencies of causes of death is useful for determining the significance of various diseases in contributing to death. As we have seen from the preceding section, certain causes are more likely to be underlying causes, like cancer, while others, like diabetes, are more likely to be nonunderlying causes. It is important to be aware of changes in the relative ranking of causes of death when the total mention of a disease is used. For example, the total mention ranking of both cancer and accidents is often lower than their underlying cause ranking. Generalized arteriosclerosis has a much higher ranking in terms of its total occurrence on the death certificate than as an underlying cause of death. In the oldest age group it is the second leading cause of death rather than being ranked fifth as an underlying cause of death (Manton and Stallard, 1984).

Sex- and race-specific mortality rates and differentials by age
for these six causes of death are shown in table 6.7. The top two
panels of the table show the rates for each sex and race, while the
lower two panels show the ratios of male to female and white to
nonwhite mortality rates. Of particular interest in the table is the
comparison of race and sex differentials when the total mention of
a cause is examined rather than the traditional underlying cause.
For example, there is a larger sex differential for each age group
when the total mention of cancer, as well as of influenza/pneu-
monia, is examined. For diseases such as stroke and diabetes,
there is a larger sex differential when total mention rates are
examined until age 85, when a reversal of the sex differential
occurs. For chronic obstructive respiratory disease (CORD), there
are larger sex differentials for the TM rates in the age group
65-74, similar sex differentials in the 75-84 age group, and smaller
sex differentials in the oldest age group. When the TM rates are
examined, heart disease, on the other hand, has slightly lower sex
differentials until age 75 and slightly higher differentials thereafter. The well-known crossover phenomenon of whites having
higher mortality than nonwhites in the older ages is observed for
the total mention rates as well as the underlying cause rates for
each cause except diabetes. The crossover occurs for the total
mention rates in the age group 85+, but not for the underlying
cause rate. However, this result is due to the open-endedness of
the oldest old age group. When data are examined for the age
groups 85-94 and 95+, one observes the crossover in the 95+
group. Race differentials are similar for stroke when the UC or
TM rates are used. Heart disease and chronic obstructive respiratory disease both have larger race differentials when the underlying cause rates are used. On the other hand, cancer and
influenza/pneumonia have larger race differentials when the total
mention rates are used.

Another way to show differentials by sex and race in multiple
causes is to compare the TM/UC ratios. These data are shown in
table 6.8. For heart disease, males have higher ratios after age 75,
and nonwhites have higher ratios in each age group. For cancer,
influenza/pneumonia, and diabetes, males and whites have higher
ratios than females and nonwhites. This pattern also holds for
stroke, except in the oldest old age group, where whites and nonwhites have similar ratios. For chronic obstructive respiratory
disease, males have higher ratios in the 65-74 age group, similar

Table 6.7
Gender- and Race-specific Mortality Rates and Differentials by Underlying Cause (UC) and Total Mentions (TM), United States, 1982 (per 100,000 persons)

		Heart Disease			Cancer			Stroke		
		65-74	75-84	85+	65-74	75-84	85+	65-74	75-84	85+
MALE	UC	1673	3630	8240	1118	1807	2420	231	740	1909
	TM	2421	5352	11926	1273	2209	3331	417	1302	3189
FEMALE	UC	811	2322	6942	635	907	1253	171	636	2038
	TM	1231	3323	9560	704	1071	1646	292	1053	3296
WHITE	UC	1171	2832	7502	832	1238	1609	183	664	2040
	TM	1709	4086	10472	939	1494	2170	323	1133	3321
OTHER	UC	1342	2514	5368	972	1234	1464	330	774	1560
	TM	2139	3897	7892	1094	1440	1837	562	1257	2551

148

Group		Influenza			Diabetes			C.O.R.D.		
MALE	UC	70	268	1018	62	128	193	206	450	584
	TM	290	859	2599	285	566	942	499	1093	1544
FEMALE	UC	32	133	630	62	125	218	78	112	143
	TM	120	405	1587	240	503	853	163	267	414
WHITE	UC	46	186	768	57	121	208	140	249	295
	TM	187	583	1951	248	522	859	323	596	779
OTHER	UC	65	155	477	110	173	236	81	110	140
	TM	217	456	1155	369	559	745	193	283	385

Group		Heart Disease			Cancer			Stroke		
MALE/	UC	2.06	1.56	1.19	1.76	1.99	1.93	1.35	1.16	0.94
FEMALE	TM	1.97	1.61	1.25	1.81	2.06	2.02	1.43	1.24	0.97
WHITE/	UC	0.87	1.13	1.40	0.86	1.00	1.10	0.55	0.86	1.31
OTHER	TM	0.80	1.05	1.33	0.87	1.04	1.18	0.57	0.90	1.30

Table 6.7 (continued)

		Influenza			Diabetes			C. O. R. D.	
	65-74	75-84	85+	65-74	75-84	85+	65-74	75-84	85+
MALE/ UC	2.19	2.01	1.62	1.01	1.02	0.88	2.64	4.00	4.09
FEMALE TM	2.33	2.12	1.64	1.19	1.13	0.99	3.07	4.05	3.73
WHITE/ UC	0.71	1.20	1.61	0.52	0.70	0.88	1.72	2.26	2.03
OTHER TM	0.86	1.28	1.69	0.67	0.93	1.15	1.67	2.10	2.03

Source: National Center for Health Statistics. Multiple-Cause-of-Death Public User Tapes

150

Table 6.8
Gender- and Race-specific Mortality Rates and Ratios of Total Mentions (TM) to Underlying Cause (UC), United States, 1982 (per 100,000 persons)

		Heart Disease			Cancer			Stroke		
		65-74	75-84	85+	65-74	75-84	85+	65-74	75-84	85+
MALE	UC	1673	3630	8240	1118	1807	2420	231	740	1909
	TM	2421	5352	11926	1273	2209	3331	417	1302	3189
FEMALE	UC	811	2322	6942	635	907	1253	171	636	2038
	TM	1231	3323	9560	704	1071	1646	292	1053	3286
WHITE	UC	1171	2832	7502	832	1238	1609	183	664	2040
	TM	1709	4096	10472	939	1494	2170	323	1133	3321
OTHER	UC	1342	2514	5368	972	1234	1464	330	774	1560
	TM	2139	3897	7982	1084	1440	1937	562	1257	2551

Table 6.8 (continued)

		Influenza			Diabetes			C.O.R.D.		
		65-74	75-84	85+	65-74	75-84	85+	65-74	75-84	85+
MALE	UC	70	268	1018	62	128	193	206	450	584
	TM	280	858	2599	285	566	842	499	1093	1544
FEMALE	UC	32	133	630	62	125	218	78	112	143
	TM	120	405	1587	240	503	853	163	267	414
WHITE	UC	46	186	768	57	121	208	140	249	285
	TM	197	583	1951	248	522	859	323	596	779
OTHER	UC	65	155	477	110	173	236	81	110	140
	TM	217	456	1155	369	559	745	193	293	385

	Heart Disease			Cancer			Stroke		
	65-74	75-84	85+	65-74	75-84	85+	65-74	75-84	85+
MALE	1.45	1.47	1.45	1.14	1.22	1.38	1.80	1.76	1.67
FEMALE	1.52	1.43	1.38	1.11	1.18	1.31	1.70	1.66	1.61
WHITE	1.46	1.44	1.40	1.13	1.21	1.35	1.77	1.71	1.63
OTHER	1.59	1.55	1.47	1.12	1.17	1.26	1.70	1.63	1.64

	Influenza			Diabetes			C.O.R.D.		
MALE	4.02	3.20	2.55	4.58	4.43	4.37	2.42	2.41	2.64
FEMALE	3.77	3.03	2.52	3.89	4.03	3.91	2.09	2.38	2.90
WHITE	4.03	3.14	2.54	4.36	4.32	4.12	2.31	2.39	2.74
OTHER	3.32	2.94	2.42	3.36	3.23	3.16	2.37	2.57	2.74

Source: National Center for Health Statistics. Multiple-Cause-of-Death Public User Tapes

153

ratios in the 75-84 age group, and lower ratios in the 85+ age group. Nonwhites have higher ratios than whites until age 85.

Cohort differentials in mortality risks are a significant component of mortality trends in the older population. Figures 6.4a and 6.4b illustrate one of the more striking observations of strong cohort differentials in mortality risks of stroke for white males. The cohort risks for stroke are consistently and rapidly declining. However, taking into account the different scales, the declines are less rapid for the multiple-cause occurrence of stroke than for its underlying cause occurrence. Persistent cohort differences suggest that much of the mortality change observed at later ages is likely to continue. This suggestion has potentially major implications for projections of future life expectancy gains in the U.S. population; that is, if recent mortality reductions in circulatory disease risks are "locked into" cohort experiences, we can expect continuing declines in those rates and increasing life expectancy at advanced ages (Manton and Myers, 1987).

Two other indicators of the health status of the older population are changes in the mean age at death and proportion of deaths because of a given cause. These data are shown in table 6.9. An increase between 1968 and 1982 in the mean age at death of over two years is observed for both UC and TM of cancer, heart disease, and stroke. Cancer had a similar rate of increase for UC and TM designations, with males having a higher rate of increase. Heart disease had a lower rate of increase for the TM designation, with males having a higher rate of increase. Cerebrovascular disease had a higher rate of increase for the TM designation, with females having a higher rate of increase.

In table 6.9, changes in the proportion of deaths expected from the cause of death after ages 65 and 85 are also shown. This value indicates the significance of a cause of death at advanced ages. Cancer decreases in importance in the oldest old age group. The total mention of heart disease and stroke increases in importance at the very advanced ages. This result is interesting given that much of the increase in life expectancy at advanced ages is being attributed to reductions to circulatory disease risks. Thus, the reduction in circulatory disease risk is a result of delays in the mean age at death to a greater extent than it is a result of decreases in the proportions of death that eventually will be due to circulatory diseases (Manton and Myers, 1987).

**Figure 6.4a
Age-specific Stroke Mortality Rates of White Male Cohorts
in the United States, Underlying Cause**

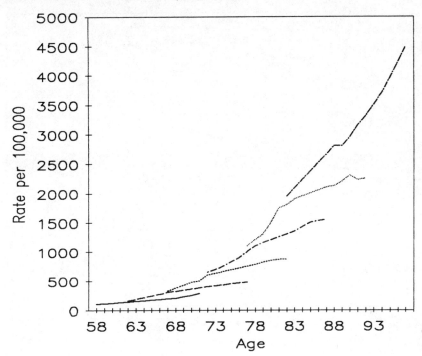

LEGEND

———— born 1909-13

—–—. born 1904-08

—————— born 1899-03

.———– born 1894-98

—————— born 1889-93

—–—– born 1884-88

Source: Adapted from Manton and Myers, 1987, p. 171.

Figure 6.4b
**Age-specific Stroke Mortality Rates of White Male Cohorts in the
United States, Total Mentions**

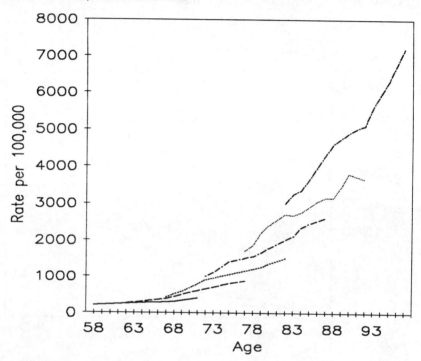

LEGEND

———— born 1909-13

—–—. born 1904-08

············ born 1899-03

·—··— born 1894-98

················ born 1889-93

——·—— born 1884-88

Source: Adapted from Manton and Myers, 1987, p. 171.

Table 6.9
Mean Time to Death and Number of Years Increase and Proportion of Deaths Caused by Cancer, Heart Disease, and Stroke, by Underlying Cause and Total Mention Occurrences, White Males and Females, United States, 1968 and 1982

		MALE			FEMALE		
		Cancer	Heart Disease	Stroke	Cancer	Heart Disease	Stroke
Mean Age at Death: 1968	UC	69.45	71.70	76.15	69.28	79.75	80.83
1968	TM	69.43	71.46	75.46	70.34	79.31	80.29
1982	UC	71.11	74.80	78.70	71.61	82.61	83.59
1982	TM	72.06	74.65	78.43	72.69	81.58	83.41
Increase, 1968-82	UC	2.66	3.10	2.55	2.33	2.86	2.76
Increase, 1968-82	TM	2.63	2.89	2.97	2.35	2.27	3.12
Proportions of Total Deaths at age 65: 1968	UC	14.27	45.92	12.40	11.05	46.51	17.18
1968	TM	17.29	57.80	19.13	13.06	58.14	25.59
1982	UC	19.30	44.02	8.15	14.17	46.62	12.55
1982	TM	23.33	63.69	14.23	16.80	65.57	20.50
Proportions of Total Deaths at age 85: 1968	UC	7.86	46.61	16.49	5.77	48.29	19.43
1968	TM	11.13	59.26	23.79	7.62	59.45	27.55
1982	UC	11.77	46.73	10.74	7.53	50.74	14.64
1982	TM	16.36	67.21	17.87	10.00	69.33	23.49

Source: National Center on Health Statistics, Multiple Cause of Death Public-Use Tapes

157

The health status of the older population, which has been described in the preceding sections, is related to but distinct from the need for and utilization of health care services. These latter components of the health status of the older population and the costs of these services will be addressed in the last sections of this chapter. Data to be presented were obtained primarily from surveys conducted by the National Center for Health Statistics (NCHS) and, in general, were published in *Health Statistics on Older Persons* (NCHS, 1987b).

The level of use of the older population not in institutions for three basic health care services is shown in table 6.10. The proportion of the population using any of these services increases with age. Slightly over 20 percent of males 65-74 and 75 + spent over two days in the hospital. Sixteen percent of females 65-74 spent over two days in the hospital compared to 23 percent for those 75 and over. It is interesting that a greater proportion of females than males 75 years and over spent over two days in the hospital. Between 80 and 90 percent of the older population required some level of ambulatory care. Seven percent of males 75 years and over had twenty or more nondental visits to a physician or other provider compared to 13 percent of females 75 years and over. Over half of the older population needed between two and twenty-four prescribed drugs. The proportion of the population requiring prescribed medication increases greatly for those under 65 to those 75 years and over. For males the proportion increases from 67 percent to 80 percent, and for females the proportion increases from 77 percent to 87 percent. In addition, 20 percent of the population 75 years and over required over two dozen prescriptions.

Selected indicators of health status and health care utilization by age group and income level are shown in table 6.11. The number of activity limitations per person in each age group decreases with income. The proportion of older persons reporting fair or poor health also decreases with income. The number of physician visits per person remains relatively constant across the income scale. The number of days spent in hospitals bears little relationship to income except for a slight decrease as income rises for persons under 75. The number of dental visits actually increases as income rises. Within income classes, it is often the case that the number of limitations in the activities of daily living and average days spent in a hospital increases with age, but this trend is not the case for self-assessed health status, where such a relationship with age

Table 6.10
Percent Distribution of Persons 55 Years of Age and Over by Level of
Hospital, Ambulatory Care, and Prescription Drug Use, by Age and
Gender, United States, 1980

Level of Usage

	None	Low	Medium	High
Hospital Use				
Male: 55-64	96.4	1.3	8.4	3.9
65-74	77.3	1.6	15.2	5.9
75+	75.1	3.1	10.7	11.1
Female: 55-64	87.6	1.4	8.6	2.3
65-74	82.7	1.6	10.8	4.9
75+	74.9	1.8	15.0	9.3
Ambulatory Care Use				
Male: 55-64	19.7	13.6	62.9	3.8
65-74	19.7	10.0	61.8	8.5
75+	16.6	9.7	67.0	6.7

Table 6.10 (continued)

Level of Usage

	None	Low	Medium	High
Ambulatory Care Use				
Female: 55-64	14.4	12.8	65.2	7.7
65-74	14.3	9.4	66.9	9.4
75+	10.2	7.2	70.1	12.5
Prescription Drug Use				
Male: 55-64	32.9	10.7	49.3	7.1
65-74	29.1	8.2	52.0	10.7
75+	19.5	4.4	59.2	18.9
Female: 55-64	23.2	7.1	59.4	12.3
65-74	19.7	5.2	60.0	15.1
75+	13.4	4.8	62.1	19.7

Source: National Center for Health Statistics (1987b), p. 58

Note: Low users had 1 or 2 hospital days, 1 physician visit and 1 prescription medication acquisition during the year; levels for high users were 17 or more hospital days, 20 or more physician visits and 25 or more prescription acquisitions.

160

Table 6.11
Selected Indicators of Health Status, by Age and Income, 1979-1980

Age Group	Total	Under $3,000	$3,000-4,999	$5,000-6,999	$7,000-9,999	$10,000-14,999	$15,000-24,999	$25,000+
			Activity Limitations per Person					
55-64	3.0	6.0	5.7	4.5	3.8	3.1	2.3	1.8
65-74	4.1	5.9	5.3	4.7	4.4	3.7	3.2	2.9
75+	5.3	6.0	5.4	5.1	5.4	5.1	5.3	5.5
			Percent in Fair or Poor Health					
55-64	26	57	50	44	37	29	18	13
65-74	32	48	43	38	33	25	21	18
75+	31	35	33	32	31	30	27	27
			Physician Visits per Person					
55-64	5.3	6.2	8.7	5.9	5.5	5.6	5.1	5.4
65-74	6.3	6.9	6.6	6.4	6.2	6.3	6.1	6.6
75+	6.6	6.2	6.1	5.9	6.1	7.2	8.3	7.2

Table 6.11 (continued)

Age Group	Total	Under $3,000	$3,000- 4,999	$5,000- 6,999	$7,000- 9,999	$10,000- 14,999	$15,000- 24,999	$25,000+
Short-stay Hospital Days per Person								
55-64	1.8	3.3	2.4	3.1	2.6	2.0	1.4	1.1
65-74	2.4	3.1	3.2	2.7	2.2	2.2	1.9	2.2
75+	3.6	4.0	3.1	3.5	3.1	4.3	3.7	4.0
Dental Visits per Person								
55-64	1.8	1.1	1.0	1.3	1.5	1.5	1.9	2.6
65-74	1.5	1.0	1.2	0.9	1.5	1.4	2.2	2.9
75+	1.2	0.9	0.9	1.0	0.9	1.6	1.1	2.5

Source: National Center for Health Statistics, 1984, p. 21

holds only at the highest income levels. For income levels below $10,000, a lower proportion of persons in the oldest age groups reports being in fair or poor health than in the youngest old groups. Physician visits generally increase with age for persons in income levels above $7,000. Dental visits, on the other hand, decrease with age at virtually all income levels.

As we have seen, the utilization of ambulatory care in the older population is high, as over 80 percent of the population seeks some level of care by physicians. Table 6.12 shows the most frequent diagnoses for ambulatory patients for each of the older age groups and their relative ranking for males and females. It is interesting to compare this table with the prevalence of chronic conditions shown in table 6.1. For example, arthritis is the most prevalent condition in the older population, yet it is only fourth in terms of ambulatory care. Hypertension is a prevalent condition in the older population and is reflected in the ambulatory care figures. Diabetes is listed as the second or third most frequent diagnosis for persons under 85, although its prevalence in the population is lower than that of other conditions. Sex differences worth mentioning are that females tend to be treated more for arthropathies and osteoarthritis, while males tend to be treated more for heart disease. Important age differences are also observed for obesity, which ranked sixth in the 55-64 age group and then drops out thereafter. Neurotic disorders are more common for persons under 75. A significant component of the health status and need of the older population is mental health services. Based on surveys conducted in 1980 by the Survey and Reports Branch, National Institute of Mental health, which sampled admissions to various psychiatric services, the estimate was that persons 65 years and older accounted for 7 percent (N = 99, 715) of the 1.3 million admissions to inpatient psychiatric services, with an admission rate of 388 per 100 thousand (Rosenstein et al., 1987).

Hospital discharges for surgical procedures are shown separately for males and females in tables 6.13 and 6.14. The most frequent surgical procedure for males 65 years and older is prostatectomy, followed by extraction of lens, repair of inguinal hernia, pacemaker insertion, and cardiac catheterization. For males under 65, repair of inguinal hernia is the most common surgical procedure. There are some noteworthy variations in this pattern when specific age groups are examined. For example, between 65 and 74, cardiac catheterization becomes the second most frequent

Table 6.12
Number of Mentions of Most Frequent All Listed Diagnoses for
Ambulatory Patients Aged 55 and Over and Rank, by Gender and
Age, United States, 1980 and 1981

Age 55-64	Mentions per 1,000 visits	Comparable Rank	
		Female	Male
Essential hypertension	167	1	1
Diabetes mellitus	66	2	3
Chronic ischemic heart disease	42	8	2
Osteoarthritis and related disorders	35	3	4
Neurotic disorders	31	4	7
Obesity	27	5	11
Arthropathies	25	6	9
Disorders of refraction/accommodation	22	9	8
Acute upper respiratory infections	19	10	14
Cardiac dysrhythmias	17	14	6

Age 65-74

Essential hypertension	192	1	1
Diabetes mellitus	78	2	3
Chronic ischemic heart disease	62	4	2
Osteoarthritis and related disorders	45	3	5
Arthropathies	31	5	12
Cataract	29	6	9
Hypertensive heart disease	24	8	8
Heart failure	24	9	6
Chronic airway obstruction	22	24	4
Neurotic disorders	20	7	26

Age 75-84

Essential hypertension	175	1	1
Chronic ischemic heart disease	91	2	2
Diabetes mellitus	70	4	3
Osteoarthritis and related disorders	57	3	9
Cataract	50	5	7
Heart failure	39	7	4
Arthropathies	36	6	14
Cardiac dysrhythmias	34	9	9
Glaucoma	28	10	13
Angina pectoris	26	11	11

Table 6.12 (continued)

Age 85+	Mentions per 1,000 visits	Comparable Rank	
		Female	Male
Essential hypertension	171	1	2
Chronic ischemic heart disease	117	2	1
Osteoarthritis and related disorders	74	3	8
Cataract	68	4	3
Heart failure	65	5	4
Diabetes mellitus	49	9	5
Cardiac dysrhythmias	47	10	6
Atherosclerosis	37	9	9
Arthropathies	37	7	13
Hypertensive heart disease	37	6	25

Source: National Center for Health Statistics (1987b), p. 59

Table 6.13
Number and Rate of Surgical Procedures for Males Aged 55 and Over
Discharged from Short-Stay Hospitals, by Age and Selected
Procedures, United States, 1979 and 1984

	Thousands of procedures		Number per 10,000	
	1979	1984	1979	1984
Age 55-64				
Repair of inguinal hernia	79	74	79	70
Cardiac Catheterization	62	118	62	113
Prostatectomy	59	70	59	67
Direct heart revascularization	39	60	39	57
Extraction of lens	32	29	31	28
Age 65-74				
Prostatectomy	122	151	183	207
Repair of inguinal hernia	72	68	108	93
Extraction of lens	56	65	85	89
Pacemaker insertion	23	40	35	55
Cardiac Catheterization	22	93	34	114

Table 6.13 (continued)

	Thousands of procedures		Number per 10,000	
	1979	1984	1979	1984
Age 75-84				
Prostatectomy	79	102	279	317
Extraction of lens	42	51	147	159
Repair of inguinal hernia	32	45	112	139
Pacemaker insertion	31	32	108	101
Cholecystectomy	14	19	49	61
Age 85+				
Prostatectomy	17	22	255	281
Extraction of lens	10	16	141	207
Repair of inguinal hernia	9	7	125	91
Pacemaker insertion	8	11	118	149
Reduction of fracture	8	9	114	113

Source: National Center for Health Statistics (1987b), p. 67

Table 6.14
Number and Rate of Surgical Procedures for Females Aged 55 and
Over Discharged from Short-Stay Hospitals, by Age and Selected
Procedures, United States, 1979 and 1984

	Thousands of procedures		Number per 10,000	
	1979	1984	1979	1984
Age 55-64				
Dilation and curettage of uterus	59	31	52	26
Cholecystectomy	55	50	48	42
Hysterectomy	47	51	42	43
Reduction of fracture	40	38	35	32
Oophorectomy/salpingo-oophorectomy	38	44	33	37
Age 65-74				
Extraction of lens	87	100	101	106
Reduction of fracture	47	56	54	60
Cholecystectomy	45	57	52	60
Hysterectomy	29	43	33	46
Cardiac Catheterization	15	57	18	60

Table 6.14 (continued)

	Thousands of procedures		Number per 10,000	
	1979	1984	1979	1984
Age 75-94				
Extraction of lens	89	136	186	252
Reduction of fracture	52	54	110	99
Pacemaker insertion	30	41	64	75
Arthoplasty and replacement of hip	29	44	62	82
Cholecystectomy	25	29	53	53
Age 85+				
Reduction of fracture	34	35	223	183
Extraction of lens	22	41	144	217
Arthoplasty and replacement of hip	17	27	112	143
Pacemaker insertion	13	16	93	83
Cholecystectomy	7	5	44	29

Source: National Center for Health Statistics (1987b), p. 68

surgical procedure in 1984, resulting from an increase of over 200 percent since 1979. Between 75 and 84, cholecystectomy becomes a frequent surgical procedure. For those 85 years old and over, reduction of fracture becomes a common procedure (see table 6.13). For females 65 years and over, extraction of lens is the most frequent surgical procedure, followed by reduction of fracture, cholecystectomy, arthroplasty and replacement of hip, and pacemaker insertion. For females under 65, diagnostic dilation and curettage of uterus is the most common procedure, although this experienced a 50 percent decline since 1979. Hysterectomy is a common procedure in the 65-74 age group, affecting 43 thousand females (see table 6.14).

Hospital discharges for nonsurgical procedures are shown separately for males and females in tables 6.15 and 6.16. Both males and females are involved in similar nonsurgical procedures, although the relative frequency differs. These procedures are cystoscopy, radioisotope scan, endoscopy of large intestine, arteriography using contrast material, diagnostic ultrasound, and CAT scan. The above order is the frequency for males in each age group in 1979. There were many changes in the relative frequency of these procedures in 1984, reflecting advances in medical technology (see table 6.15). For females, the CAT scan and radioisotope scan are the most common nonsurgical procedures (see table 6.16).

With the increase occurring in the older population, particularly in the oldest old, there is a corresponding concern about providing long-term care in the home, in the community, or in an institution. The number and rate of nursing home residents by age and sex between 1973-74 and 1985 are shown in table 6.17. The number of residents 65 years and over increased from 961,500 in 1973-74 to 1,315,800 in 1985 (37 percent), but the rate remained constant at 45-46 per 1,000. Utilization rates increase markedly with age, with the oldest old having the highest rates at 219.4 per 1,000 in 1985. The utilization rates of whites and blacks and males and females are similar until age 75, but differ thereafter; whites then have higher rates than blacks, while females have higher rates than males. The rates for whites decreased between 1973-74 and 1985 while the rates for blacks increased over this period.

The comparative health care costs for the older population are shown in table 6.18. Between 1965 and 1981, the share of the nation's health care expenditures for the benefit of the older population increased from 25 percent to 33 percent. The older popula-

Table 6.15
Number and Rate of Diagnostic and Other Nonsurgical Procedures
for Male Hospital Discharges 55 Years of Age and Over, by Age
and Selected Procedures, United States, 1979 and 1984

	Thousands of procedures		Number per 10,000	
	1979	1984	1979	1984
Age 55-64				
Cystoscopy	99	95	99	91
Angiocardiography using contrast material	54	107	54	102
Radioisotope scan	52	71	52	68
Arteriography using contrast material	47	64	47	61
Endoscopy of large intestine	45	43	45	42
CAT scan	17	87	17	83
Age 65-74				
Cystoscopy	145	163	218	223
Radioisotope scan	60	84	90	115
Endoscopy of large intestine	51	66	77	90
Arteriography using contrast material	46	75	69	102
Diagnostic ultrasound	21	70	32	96
CAT scan	20	109	31	149

Age 75-84

Cystoscopy	90	127	317	397
Radioisotope scan	36	67	127	209
Endoscopy of large intestine	26	56	93	174
Arteriography using contrast material	12	48	44	150
Diagnostic ultrasound	11	56	40	175
CAT scan	10	88	36	274

Age 85+

Cystoscopy	25	26	365	337
Radioisotope scan	9	21	130	267
Endoscopy of large intestine	6	13	94	166
Diagnostic ultrasound	3	14	46	175
CAT scan	2	27	36	353
Endoscopy of small intestine	2	12	30	159

Source: National Center for Health Statistics (1997b), p. 69

173

Table 6.16
Number and Rate of Diagnostic and Other Nonsurgical Procedures
for Female Hospital Discharges 55 Years of Age and Over, by Age
and Selected Procedures, United States, 1979 and 1984

	Thousands of procedures		Number per 10,000	
	1979	1984	1979	1984
Age 55-64				
Radioisotope scan	53	80	48	67
Cystoscopy	52	34	46	29
Endoscopy of large intestine	50	64	44	54
Arteriography using contrast material	31	47	27	40
Angiocardiography using contrast material	23	56	20	48
CAT scan	16	92	14	79
Age 65-74				
Radioisotope scan	67	95	77	101
Endoscopy of large intestine	58	88	67	93
Cystoscopy	52	42	60	44
Arteriography using contrast material	34	66	39	71
Diagnostic ultrasound	19	80	22	85
CAT scan	19	116	22	123

Age 75-84

Radioisotope scan	47	82	98	152
Endoscopy of large intestine	43	80	90	148
Cystoscopy	34	34	71	62
Arteriogram using contrast material	15	35	31	65
CAT scan	12	123	25	228
Diagnostic ultrasound	11	94	24	155

Age 85+

Radioisotope scan	13	31	87	161
Endoscopy of large intestine	11	32	75	170
Cystoscopy	11	11	70	59
Diagnostic ultrasound	4	29	28	152
CAT scan	3	38	22	199
Endoscopy of small intestine	3	23	22	121

Source: National Center for Health Statistics (1987b), p. 70

Table 6.17
Number and Rate of Nursing Home Residents 55 Years of Age and Over, by Gender, Age, and Race, United States, 1973-1974, 1977, and 1985

	Thousands of Residents			Number per 1,000 persons		
	1973-4	1977	1985	1973-4	1977	1985
Total						
55-64	62.5	100.8	91.8	3.2	4.3	4.1
65-74	163.1	211.4	212.1	12.3	14.5	12.5
75-84	384.9	464.7	509.0	59.4	68.0	57.7
85+	413.6	449.9	594.7	253.7	216.4	219.4
White Male						
55-64	23.7	38.4	34.4	2.9	4.4	3.7
65-74	59.1	69.4	70.6	11.4	12.2	10.5
75-84	97.5	115.8	127.6	42.5	49.4	42.9
85+	94.2	87.3	104.6	191.1	149.7	150.4

Black Male

55-64	3.3	4.6	8.7	4.4	5.7	9.3
65-74	5.4	9.2	3.9	11.0	16.5	14.5
75-84	4.0	5.4	11.7	21.4	29.3	45.6
85+	3.8	4.2	6.2	93.8	70.0	95.6

White Female

55-64	32.1	51.8	41.8	3.5	5.4	4.0
65-74	91.0	118.1	117.2	13.4	15.8	13.7
75-84	272.2	327.4	346.0	73.9	93.3	69.6
85+	306.6	341.8	458.9	307.5	264.6	258.0

Black Female

55-64	2.9	5.7	4.8	3.2	5.9	4.2
65-74	6.9	12.8	13.5	11.0	17.6	16.0
75-84	9.4	14.4	18.9	36.0	51.6	45.1
85+	8.3	14.9	22.8	103.5	125.2	162.7

Source: National Center for Health Statistics (1987b), p. 73

Table 6.18
Aggregate Health Care Expenditures for Persons Aged 65 and Over
by Type of Service and Source, 1965, 1970, 1976, and 1981

(millions of dollars)

Type	Total for Elderly	Percent of total for all ages	Private Funds	Public Funds	Percent Public
1965					
Physicians Services	$1,737	20.5%	$1,617	$120	6.9%
Hospitals	$3,296	23.6%	$1,677	$1,619	49.1%
Drugs	$1,148	20.0%	$1,030	$118	10.3%
Nursing Homes	$1,825	88.1%	$1,187	$638	35.0%
Other	$963	11.3%	$702	$161	18.7%
Total	$8,869	23.4%	$6,213	$2,656	29.9%
1970					
Physicians Services	$3,030	21.1%	$1,166	$1,864	61.5%
Hospitals	$7,054	27.2%	$806	$6,248	88.6%
Drugs	$1,732	21.2%	$1,524	$208	12.0%
Nursing Homes	$4,144	89.6%	$2,255	$1,889	45.6%
Other	$1,310	12.5%	$943	$367	28.0%
Total	$17,270	26.3%	$6,694	$10,576	61.2%

1976

Physicians				
Services	$6,505	23.5%	$2,746	$3,759	57.8%
Hospitals	$16,305	27.2%	$1,831	$14,474	88.8%
Drugs	$2,716	21.2%	$2,263	$453	16.7%
Nursing Homes	$9,395	82.0%	$4,693	$4,702	50.0%
Other	$2,753	13.4%	$1,839	$914	33.2%
Total	$37,674	28.5%	$13,372	$24,302	64.5%

1991

Physicians				
Services	$15,600	28.5%	$6,600	$9,000	57.7%
Hospitals	$36,600	31.0%	$5,300	$31,300	85.5%
Drugs	$5,100	23.8%	$4,200	$900	17.6%
Nursing Homes	$19,400	80.1%	$9,600	$9,800	50.5%
Other	$6,500	17.7%	$4,300	$2,200	33.8%
Total	$93,200	32.6%	$30,000	$53,200	63.9%

Source: Rabin, 1985, p. 43

179

tion accounted for nearly all long-term care expenditures, although this proportion decreased from 88 percent to 80 percent between 1965 and 1981. The share of expenditures on physician fees, hospital charges, and pharmaceuticals for the benefit of the older population was similar and increased gradually over time. The most striking change observed is the shift of health care expenditures from private to public funds. The introduction of the Medicare program in 1965 created a reversal of the distribution of the source of funds. Public funds now account for nearly two-thirds of health care expenditures for the older population compared to 30 percent in 1965.

7

Policy Implications

There is clearly a very large set of policy implications that may be drawn from the analyses and discussion that have been presented in this book. Our intention here will not be to endeavor to discuss all or even most of these, but rather to focus on a set of issues that seem to us to be most compelling. The general perspective that will be adopted with regard to policy questions is a division along two principal axes of interest. The first of these has to do with the nature of the demographic change in question. By this, we mean whether the focus is on the question of (1) the increase in the absolute number of older persons in the population; (2) the increase in the share of the population that may be considered as being older; or (3) the structural change within the older population or, more specifically, the aging of the older population itself, which seems inevitable under most reasoned assessments of the demographic future of the United States. The second axis of consideration will principally reflect whether the concern is with the well-being (from whatever perspective) of older individuals or whether the concern is for the collective well-being of society as a whole. Many questions will, of course, contain elements that cut across this rather simple demarcation.

As a general statement, it seems reasonable to assert that the increases in the number of older persons necessarily imply increases in the demand for those goods and services that are disproportionately consumed by older persons. Although one could

identify a variety of such items, it would seem that the most salient area for consideration is health care, including long-term
care. As noted previously in this book, the elderly consume relatively large amounts of health care, and it is also the case that
much of the expenditures on care are made by or on behalf of persons in their last year of life. With the compositional changes in
the older population, there is every likelihood that the demand for
health care will rise at a rate that exceeds the rate of increase of
the older population (Torrey, 1985). The prolongation of life or the
so-called rectangularization of mortality suggests the real possibility that a significant portion of these additional years will be
marked by prolonged periods of chronic morbidity and/or disability. This situation would serve to exacerbate the demand for
publicly funded health care without adding to the ability of society
to pay for this care. Figure 7.1 illustrates the rectangularization of
mortality.

One must recognize that the increase in the number of older persons carries with it an inevitable increase in the number of persons
who will be entitled to publicly funded retirement and survivors
benefits under the provisions of Social Security. Both the retire-
ment/survivors program and the health care program are funded
through a pay-as-you-go mechanism. The problems inherent in
this mechanism are properly viewed as a response not to the
increased number of older persons in the population, but to the
increased share of the total population that the elderly will
represent. More specifically, the decline in the prospective number
of economically active persons relative to the number of persons
eligible for retirement and health care benefits is at the heart of
the issue.

Because of a failure to recognize that the relative number of
economically inactive persons at the other end of the age spectrum
will diminish, one can argue that it is easy to overstate the extent
to which this issue might be problematic. On the surface, it would
seem simple to argue that the increased costs for the old will be
offset by the decreased costs of the young, particularly with
regard to their educational needs. Upon closer examination, however, there are several problems inherent in this line of reasoning.
First, it is not a simple administrative matter to transfer funds
between education, on the one hand, and health or pension
systems, on the other. In the specific context of the United States,
the former is largely the province of state and local governments,

Figure 7.1
Proportion of White Female Birth Cohorts Surviving to Specified Ages (Period Data)

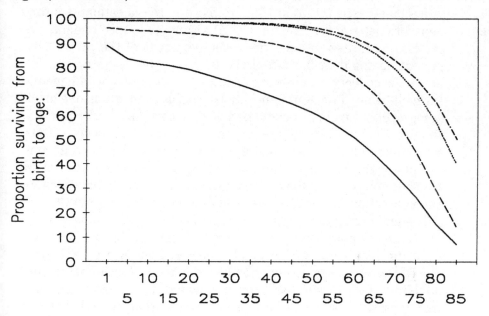

LEGEND
_____ 1900
_ _ _ . 1940
.... 1985
.__.__. 2005

Source: Spencer, 1989, p. 147; U.S. National Center for Health Statistics, 1988, p. 12.

while the latter is under the aegis of the national government. Second, the level of per capita public expenditures for the elderly tends to exceed that for youth by a factor of nearly 3 to 1 in economically advanced nations (van den Boomen, 1981). Thus, even if the increase in the number of elderly were exactly offset by a decrease in the number of youth (and this possibility is far from being the case), there would be a much greater increase in the prospective level of age-related public expenditure than there would be in the number of economically active persons to underwrite these expenditures. Finally, there is the question of intergenerational equity. Preston (1984) argues that the tendency in the United States to meet the collective needs of the present by increasing the debt burden of the future is short-sighted and ignores the collective well-being of future generations by enhancing the well-being of present generations. In this connection, one must recognize that from a societal perspective there are important differences in the outcomes of expenditures for the elderly versus those for children. The former are properly viewed as current consumption while the latter are, at least in part, properly viewed as being (human) capital formation and therefore likely to have longer-run consequences for the level and rate of economic growth.

The entire question of the connection between economic growth and population aging is one that has concerned scholars for much of the present century (Clark and Spengler, 1980; Serow, 1975) but one which remains quite imperfectly understood. Much of our understanding of this issue has been predicated upon the assumption that population size will be more or less stationary and that the economic outcome of this assumption is relatively favorable. It is only recently that attention has come to be paid on the possibility of population decline, the economic ramifications of which are thought to be not nearly so sanguine (Davis, Bernstam, and Ricardo-Campbell, 1986; Serow, 1984; Teitelbaum and Winter, 1985). Even in the context of the United States, where immigration is likely to preclude the onset of immediate population decline, much more attention needs to be paid to the policy consequences of the dramatic aging of the older population that is likely to occur after the year 2025.

From the discussion at the beginning of this book, one could identify three phases that will characterize the aging of the American population during the next 100 years. During the first phase, until the end of the present century, the growth of the older population will occur at a historically modest pace, with much of the growth likely to be concentrated among the very old. Because the economically active population will be increasing in size and collectively reaching the years of peak lifetime earnings, there should be little problem in terms of pension funding; health care funding may be somewhat more problematic owing to the increase in the size of the oldest old. During the second phase of the process, from about the turn of the century until about 2025, both the number and the share of the elderly in the population will increase rapidly, but the aging of the older population will temporarily halt because of the attainment of age 60 by the baby boom cohorts. During this period, there will be relatively more pressure on pension funding, but (compared with preceding and succeeding periods) relatively less pressure on health care funding. Finally, increases in both the number and share of the elderly in the population will level out after 2025, but the number and the proportion of the population aged 85 and over will more than double between that year and 2080. Once again, during this period the crucial funding issues may well revolve around health care. However, in contrast to the present, the growth of the oldest old in the twenty-first century will not be counterbalanced by expansion of the economically active population. During the fifty-five-year period beginning in 2025, the size of the American population will diminish by some 6 million persons if one accepts the midlevel mortality assumption or increase by nearly 10 million under lower levels of mortality; the size of the population aged 85 and over will expand by either 10.0 or 21.2 million persons during this same period, depending upon assumptions regarding mortality. As is shown in figures 7.2a and 7.2b, this analysis connotes that the population will decline at all ages under 85 years under mid-level mortality or at all ages under 80 under low mortality. In either case, it is only at ages 45 to 59 and, especially, from 70 and onward that there would be any growth of population.

By way of conclusion, the policy implications of population aging seem to depend very much upon the temporal horizon under consideration. For the immediate future, that is, over the next thirty-five to forty years, it would seem that prudent policymakers will be able to cope with increased demand for publicly provided health and pension services without a great deal of difficulty. Although that segment of the population most likely to require substantial health and long-term care services will expand rapidly, the fiscal

Figure 7.2a
Population Change by Age, Low and Medium Mortality Variants,
2025-2080

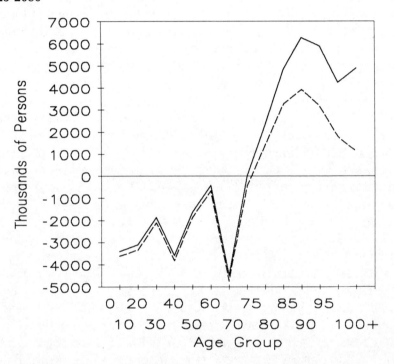

LEGEND

_____ Low Mortality

_ _ _. Medium Mortality

Source: Spencer, 1989, pp. 107, 110.

Figure 7.2b
Cumulative Population Change by Age, Low and Medium Mortality
Variants, 2025-2080

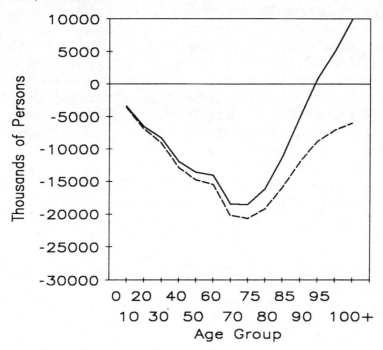

base required to pay for such services should also expand as the number of persons at or near their peak lifetime earnings continues to grow. While these individuals will experience increased earnings and savings capacity, it is also the case that many of these persons in either their late middle or their young old years will have oldest old parents who may require financial support. Thus, the level of savings, which is critical to sustain economic growth, might be somewhat less than might be anticipated.

In the longer run, the demographic situation may prove even more problematic. The combination of the pronounced increase in the number and share of persons in the population aged 60 and above and the dramatic aging of this population produces a scenario that will require an extraordinary level of foresight and an extraordinary set of policies that will have to be determined and set into place before these long-run changes are well underway. Among the most salient policy concerns should be the encouragement of labor force participation by as many capable and interested persons as possible regardless of age; the possible encouragement and facilitation of additional immigration as a means of mitigating the potentially adverse economic consequences of population decline; the development of programs to enhance the economic well-being of all older persons regardless of their demographic characteristics; and the development of mechanisms to permit older persons to remain in their own home for as long as possible and to prevent them from being placed in institutions unless absolutely necessary. Clearly, much additional research is needed both to uncover the long-range implications of prospective population change and to assess the comparative outcomes of alternative policy measures. However, measures of the general type outlined here should promote a favorable outcome for future generations of older Americans and for the society of which they will be an integral part.

APPENDIX

A-1
International Comparisons of Population Aging: Percent of Total Population above
Specified Age, 1965-2025

	1965 Total, All Ages (000s)	1965 percent: 65+	75+	80+	1985 Total, All Ages (000s)	1985 percent: 65+	75+	80+
United States	194,303	9.5%	3.4%	1.6%	238,631	12.0%	4.9%	2.6%
Austria	7,255	13.3%	4.5%	2.0%	7,502	14.1%	6.5%	3.0%
Belgium	9,464	12.6%	4.4%	2.0%	9,903	13.4%	5.9%	2.9%
Denmark	4,758	11.3%	4.0%	1.8%	5,122	14.9%	6.3%	3.2%
France	48,758	12.1%	4.5%	2.1%	54,621	12.4%	6.2%	3.2%
West Germany	59,012	11.9%	3.9%	1.7%	60,877	14.5%	6.8%	3.2%
Greece	8,551	8.9%	3.2%	1.5%	9,878	13.1%	5.5%	2.6%
Italy	51,944	9.9%	3.5%	1.6%	57,300	13.0%	5.5%	2.5%
Luxembourg	332	11.8%	3.9%	1.7%	363	12.7%	5.2%	2.3%
Norway	3,723	12.0%	4.2%	2.0%	4,142	15.5%	6.4%	3.2%
Sweden	7,734	12.7%	4.5%	2.1%	8,351	16.9%	7.2%	3.5%
United Kingdom	54,520	12.0%	4.3%	2.0%	56,125	15.1%	6.3%	3.1%

Bulgaria	8,201	8.4%	2.6%	1.0%	9,071	11.3%	4.3%	1.8%
Hungary	10,148	10.3%	3.2%	1.3%	10,697	12.5%	5.1%	2.2%
Poland	31,496	6.8%	2.0%	.8%	37,187	9.4%	4.0%	1.7%
Australia	11,387	8.5%	3.0%	1.3%	15,698	10.1%	3.7%	1.7%
Canada	19,644	7.7%	2.9%	1.4%	25,426	10.4%	4.0%	2.0%
Japan	98,891	6.2%	1.9%	.8%	120,742	10.0%	3.7%	1.7%
New Zealand	2,628	8.1%	3.0%	1.4%	3,318	10.4%	3.9%	1.8%
Bangladesh	58,373	3.8%	1.0%	.4%	101,147	3.1%	.9%	.3%
Brazil	84,292	3.2%	.9%	.3%	135,564	4.3%	1.3%	.6%
China	715,546	3.6%	.8%	.3%	1,043,204	5.1%	1.4%	.5%
Guatemala	4,568	2.7%	.8%	.3%	7,963	2.9%	.9%	.4%
Hong Kong	3,692	3.2%	.8%	.2%	5,548	7.6%	2.4%	1.0%
India	495,156	3.5%	.8%	.3%	758,927	4.3%	1.1%	.4%
Indonesia	107,041	3.1%	.8%	.3%	166,440	3.5%	.9%	.3%
Israel	2,563	5.8%	1.5%	.5%	4,252	8.9%	3.6%	1.5%
Mexico	43,500	3.4%	1.1%	.5%	78,996	3.5%	1.3%	.6%
Philippines	32,492	3.0%	1.0%	.4%	54,499	3.4%	1.0%	.4%
Singapore	1,890	2.7%	.8%	.3%	2,559	5.2%	1.6%	.6%
Uruguay	2,693	8.4%	3.0%	1.4%	3,012	10.7%	4.0%	1.9%

A-1 (continued)

| | 2005 | | | | 2025 | | | |
	Total, All Ages (000s)	percent: 65+	75+	80+	Total, All Ages (000s)	percent: 65+	75+	80+
United States	275,677	13.1%	6.7%	4.1%	301,394	19.5%	8.5%	4.8%
Austria	7,493	15.6%	6.8%	3.5%	7,279	19.7%	9.2%	4.3%
Belgium	10,019	15.9%	6.9%	3.4%	10,054	19.8%	7.9%	3.8%
Denmark	5,034	15.8%	7.2%	4.0%	4,690	22.2%	10.1%	5.0%
France	57,618	14.8%	6.4%	3.1%	58,431	19.3%	7.9%	3.6%
West Germany	58,456	18.9%	7.5%	3.8%	53,490	22.5%	9.5%	5.3%
Greece	10,564	16.9%	7.0%	3.3%	10,789	17.8%	7.9%	4.2%
Italy	58,736	16.9%	7.0%	3.4%	57,178	19.6%	9.6%	4.3%
Luxembourg	355	16.1%	6.3%	2.8%	339	21.3%	9.3%	4.1%
Norway	4,221	14.8%	7.3%	4.2%	4,261	20.2%	9.6%	4.1%
Sweden	8,079	17.2%	8.2%	4.7%	7,707	22.2%	10.5%	5.2%
United Kingdom	56,230	15.3%	6.9%	3.8%	55,919	19.7%	8.1%	4.0%

Bulgaria	9,650	15.2%	6.1%	2.8%	10,070	16.7%	7.1%	3.4%
Hungary	10,729	15.0%	6.2%	2.9%	10,598	19.0%	7.5%	0.7%
Poland	41,940	12.3%	4.9%	2.2%	45,286	17.1%	6.1%	2.7%
Australia	13,496	11.4%	4.8%	2.4%	22,575	15.9%	6.2%	2.9%
Canada	29,832	12.5%	5.6%	3.0%	33,261	18.8%	7.5%	0.7%
Japan	132,045	16.5%	6.4%	3.0%	132,082	20.3%	10.0%	4.9%
New Zealand	3,867	11.2%	4.8%	2.4%	4,202	16.3%	6.3%	2.9%
Bangladesh	161,427	2.9%	.8%	.3%	219,383	4.3%	1.1%	.4%
Brazil	193,603	5.8%	2.1%	1.0%	245,809	9.3%	3.2%	1.5%
China	1,246,396	7.4%	2.4%	1.0%	1,388,431	12.8%	4.1%	1.8%
Guatemala	13,971	3.8%	1.3%	.6%	21,668	4.9%	1.7%	.8%
Hong Kong	7,019	10.3%	4.3%	2.1%	7,617	17.5%	5.3%	2.6%
India	1,024,634	6.1%	1.8%	.7%	1,228,829	9.7%	3.1%	1.3%
Indonesia	225,597	5.6%	1.6%	.6%	272,744	9.7%	2.7%	1.2%
Israel	5,625	8.3%	3.5%	1.8%	6,865	11.9%	4.7%	2.1%
Mexico	118,876	4.6%	1.6%	.8%	154,085	7.7%	2.6%	1.2%
Philippines	80,220	4.2%	1.2%	.5%	102,787	7.5%	2.1%	.9%
Singapore	3,048	8.2%	2.7%	1.1%	3,323	17.9%	5.6%	2.2%
Uruguay	3,475	12.1%	5.0%	2.5%	3,875	12.3%	5.0%	2.7%

Source: Torrey, Kinsella and Taeuber (1987), p. 46-47

A-2
International Comparisons of Population Aging: Average Annual Percent Change in
Total Population above Specified Age, 1985-2005 and 2005-2025

	1985 to 2005			2005 to 2025		
	55-64	65-74	75+	55-64	65-74	75+
United States	1.4%	.3%	2.3%	1.2%	3.1%	1.6%
Austria	.5%	.7%	.3%	1.0%	1.2%	.8%
Belgium	.1%	1.1%	.7%	.8%	1.3%	.8%
Denmark	1.5%	0.0%	.6%	0.0%	1.3%	1.3%
France	.6%	1.3%	.5%	.7%	1.5%	1.1%
West Germany	.5%	1.8%	.2%	.8%	.2%	.9%
Greece	-.1%	1.5%	1.6%	1.3%	.2%	.6%
Italy	.1%	1.4%	1.6%	1.1%	.5%	.7%
Luxembourg	.8%	1.6%	.9%	.3%	.8%	1.1%
Norway	1.0%	-.9%	.7%	.7%	2.2%	.9%
Sweden	1.1%	-.6%	.4%	-.2%	1.1%	1.1%
United Kingdom	.4%	-.3%	.3%	.8%	1.2%	1.0%

Bulgaria	-.1%	1.8%	2.3%	.1%	.3%	.7%
Hungary	.2%	1.0%	1.0%	-.5%	1.2%	.8%
Poland	.7%	2.4%	1.8%	.6%	2.2%	1.3%
Australia	1.7%	1.2%	2.2%	1.6%	2.7%	2.2%
Canada	1.8%	1.2%	2.2%	1.2%	3.0%	2.3%
Japan	2.1%	2.7%	2.9%	-.8%	.2%	2.5%
New Zealand	1.5%	.4%	1.4%	2.0%	2.9%	2.2%
Bangladesh	2.4%	2.3%	1.7%	4.0%	3.5%	3.1%
Brazil	2.8%	3.0%	4.0%	3.2%	3.6%	0.3%
China	2.0%	2.5%	3.4%	3.9%	3.4%	3.2%
Guatemala	3.5%	4.4%	5.0%	2.9%	3.0%	3.2%
Hong Kong	1.9%	2.1%	3.7%	2.3%	3.6%	2.3%
India	2.2%	2.6%	2.7%	3.2%	3.5%	4.8%
Indonesia	2.3%	3.2%	3.2%	3.6%	3.5%	4.5%
Israel	2.0%	1.1%	1.3%	2.2%	2.9%	2.4%
Mexico	3.3%	3.4%	0.3%	4.1%	4.0%	0.7%
Philippines	3.7%	3.3%	3.6%	0.3%	3.7%	3.6%
Singapore	3.5%	3.1%	3.4%	2.1%	4.4%	4.2%
Uruguay	0.0%	.9%	1.9%	1.6%	.7%	.5%

Source: Torrey, Kinsella and Taeuber (1987), p. 50-51

A-3
U.S. Elderly by Age, Alternative Mortality Assumptions, 1990-2080

(thousands of persons)

Mid Mortality

	1990	2000	2010	2020	2030	2040	2050	2080
60-64	10,741	10,699	16,171	20,276	17,675	16,729	18,425	17,481
65-69	10,251	9,491	12,163	17,467	18,958	15,843	17,325	16,951
70-74	8,122	8,752	8,876	13,506	17,030	14,965	14,265	14,977
75-79	6,105	7,282	6,913	8,981	13,023	14,260	12,042	12,820
80-84	3,928	4,735	5,295	5,462	8,464	10,790	9,613	9,917
85-89	2,065	2,903	3,554	3,459	4,633	6,881	7,670	7,681
90-94	873	1,302	1,759	2,061	2,230	3,619	4,775	5,160
95-99	260	417	631	864	903	1,305	2,066	2,685
100+	56	100	171	266	363	446	775	1,440
Total	42,301	45,581	55,533	72,342	83,279	94,838	86,956	89,112
Percent Change		3.92%	13.06%	13.94%	4.57%	1.87%	2.50%	2.48%
Mean Age	71.7	72.7	72.0	71.6	72.8	74.3	74.5	75.1

Low Mortality

	1990	2000	2010	2020	2030	2040	2050	2080
60-64	10,757	10,846	16,620	21,000	19,372	17,426	19,229	18,331
65-69	10,270	9,663	12,633	18,369	20,074	16,845	19,464	18,188
70-74	8,142	8,957	9,341	14,485	18,486	16,360	15,670	16,635
75-79	6,125	7,509	7,402	9,898	14,638	16,250	13,853	15,013
80-84	3,843	4,919	5,775	6,219	9,940	12,974	11,750	12,525

	1990	2000	2010	2020	2030	2040	2050	2080
85-89	2,076	2,941	3,972	4,117	5,791	8,935	10,270	10,865
90-94	981	1,401	2,061	2,627	3,058	5,253	7,266	8,545
95-99	265	482	834	1,271	1,465	2,289	3,357	5,626
100+	58	132	295	545	865	1,205	2,266	5,602
Total	42,417	46,850	58,930	78,501	92,689	97,536	102,625	111,330
Percent Change		5.48%	14.76%	15.15%	6.02%	5.23%	5.22%	8.48%
Mean Age	71.7	72.9	72.4	72.1	73.6	75.4	76.1	77.6

Percent Difference

	1990	2000	2010	2020	2030	2040	2050	2080
60-64	.1%	1.4%	2.8%	3.6%	3.9%	4.2%	4.4%	4.9%
65-69	.2%	1.8%	3.9%	5.2%	5.9%	6.0%	6.6%	7.3%
70-74	.2%	2.3%	5.2%	7.2%	8.5%	9.3%	9.8%	11.1%
75-79	.3%	3.1%	7.1%	10.2%	12.4%	14.0%	15.0%	17.1%
80-84	.4%	3.9%	9.1%	13.9%	17.4%	20.2%	22.2%	26.3%
85-89	.5%	4.9%	11.8%	19.0%	25.0%	29.9%	33.9%	41.5%
90-94	.9%	7.6%	17.2%	27.5%	37.1%	45.2%	52.2%	65.6%
95-99	1.9%	15.6%	32.2%	47.1%	62.2%	75.3%	86.7%	109.5%
100+	3.6%	32.0%	72.5%	104.9%	138.3%	170.2%	192.4%	289.0%
Total	.3%	2.8%	6.1%	8.6%	11.3%	15.0%	18.0%	24.9%
Percent Change	.0%	39.7%	13.0%	8.7%	31.8%	179.3%	109.0%	242.1%
Mean Age	.0%	.2%	.5%	.8%	1.0%	1.5%	2.1%	3.3%

197

Source: Spencer, 1989, p. 107 and 110

A-4
Age Composition of High, Medium, and Low Net Immigration Series

Age	High		Interim Middle		Ultimate Middle		Low	
	Number (000s)	percent	Number (000s)	percent	Number (000s)	percent	Number (000s)	percent
0-4	93.8	11.7%	74.9	12.5%	65.7	13.1%	51.1	17.0%
5-9	75.4	9.4%	56.2	9.4%	46.0	9.2%	31.1	10.4%
10-14	55.2	6.9%	41.5	6.9%	34.5	6.9%	19.9	6.6%
15-19	91.3	11.4%	67.0	11.2%	53.0	10.6%	31.3	10.4%
20-24	167.1	20.9%	121.8	20.3%	95.5	19.1%	58.8	19.6%
25-29	143.8	18.0%	108.6	18.1%	93.4	18.7%	61.1	20.4%
30-34	71.1	8.9%	54.4	9.1%	48.0	9.6%	27.8	9.3%
35-39	32.6	4.1%	24.5	4.1%	21.4	4.3%	9.3	3.1%
40-44	24.6	3.1%	18.6	3.1%	16.1	3.2%	8.0	2.7%

Age								
45-49	15.9	2.0%	11.7	1.9%	9.9	2.0%	4.0	1.3%
50-54	13.0	1.6%	9.9	1.7%	8.6	1.7%	3.8	1.3%
55-59	12.1	1.5%	9.3	1.6%	8.4	1.7%	4.0	1.3%
60-64	9.9	1.2%	7.3	1.2%	6.8	1.4%	3.1	1.0%
65-69	5.8	.7%	4.1	.7%	3.7	.7%	1.0	.3%
70-74	1.4	.2%	.9	.2%	.6	.1%	-1.1	-.4%
75-79	-1.2	-.2%	-1.1	-.2%	-1.5	-.3%	-2.5	-.8%
80-84	-3.4	-.4%	-2.8	-.5%	-3.0	-.6%	-3.4	-1.1%
85-89	-9.7	-1.1%	-7.0	-1.2%	-7.1	-1.4%	-7.3	-2.4%
90-94	.1	.0%	.1	.0%	.1	.0%	.1	.0%
95-99	.1	.0%	.1	.0%	.1	.0%	.1	.0%
100+	0.0	0.0%	0.0	0.0%	0.0	0.0%	0.0	0.0%
Total	799.9	100.0%	600.0	100.0%	500.2	100.0%	300.2	100.0%

Source: Spencer, 1989, p. 155-162

* - for 1987-88

** - after 1997

199

A-5
Migration Flows between Regions, by Age, Northeast, 1955-1960,
1965-1970, and 1975-1980

1955-60:	Movers from other regions:				Percent from other regions:		
	Persons	Midwest	South	West	Midwest	South	West
60-64	2,025,649	4,276	7,115	1,878	.21%	.35%	.09%
65-69	1,724,524	3,905	6,105	1,577	.23%	.35%	.09%
70-74	1,274,872	2,733	4,941	1,268	.21%	.39%	.10%
75+	1,407,602	3,738	6,023	1,504	.27%	.43%	.11%
75-79	781,519	1,873	2,969	750	.24%	.38%	.10%
80-84	400,084	1,308	2,083	517	.33%	.52%	.13%
85+	225,999	617	971	237	.27%	.43%	.10%
TOTAL	6,432,647	14,712	24,184	6,227	.23%	.38%	.10%

		Movers from other regions:			Percent from other regions:		
1965-70:	Persons	Midwest	South	West	Midwest	South	West
60-64	2,260,511	4,949	7,196	2,621	.22%	.32%	.12%
65-69	1,797,940	3,692	6,526	1,926	.21%	.36%	.11%
70-74	1,435,440	2,645	5,681	1,630	.18%	.40%	.11%
75+	1,976,860	4,334	8,970	2,100	.22%	.45%	.11%
75-79	1,007,884	1,988	4,426	919	.20%	.44%	.09%
80-84	586,620	1,279	2,545	659	.22%	.43%	.11%
85+	382,356	1,067	1,999	522	.28%	.52%	.14%
TOTAL	7,470,751	15,620	28,373	8,277	.21%	.38%	.11%

		Movers from other regions:			Percent from other regions:		
1975-90:	Persons	Midwest	South	West	Midwest	South	West
60-64	2,473,398	4,348	10,116	2,851	.18%	.41%	.12%
65-69	2,090,877	3,517	9,406	2,609	.17%	.45%	.12%
70-74	1,614,154	2,249	7,533	1,815	.14%	.47%	.11%
75+	2,414,654	4,706	15,499	3,364	.19%	.64%	.14%
TOTAL	8,593,083	14,819	42,554	10,639	.17%	.50%	.12%

Source: 1960 to 1990 Censuses of Population

A-6
Migration Flows between Regions, by Age, Midwest, 1955-1960, 1965-1970, and 1975-1980

	Movers from other regions:				Percent from other regions:		
1955-60:	Persons	Northeast	South	West	Northeast	South	West
60-64	2,129,571	4,999	13,000	6,634	.23%	.61%	.31%
65-69	1,857,531	4,415	9,747	6,370	.24%	.52%	.34%
70-74	1,420,344	3,615	7,213	4,922	.25%	.51%	.35%
75+	1,690,313	4,067	9,354	5,776	.24%	.56%	.34%
75-79	925,313	2,292	4,840	3,181	.25%	.52%	.34%
80-84	480,267	1,028	2,744	1,718	.21%	.57%	.36%
85+	274,733	747	1,770	877	.27%	.64%	.32%
TOTAL	7,096,759	16,996	39,314	23,702	.24%	.55%	.33%

Movers from other regions: Percent from other regions:

1965-70:	Persons	Northeast	South	West	Northeast	South	West
60-64	2,378,576	4,503	12,651	9,183	.19%	.53%	.39%
65-69	1,909,704	4,645	10,373	7,915	.24%	.54%	.41%
70-74	1,536,549	3,276	8,327	5,454	.21%	.54%	.35%
75+	2,287,715	5,543	14,293	8,111	.24%	.62%	.35%
75-79	1,143,631	2,548	6,562	3,784	.22%	.57%	.33%
80-84	689,207	1,801	4,360	2,449	.26%	.63%	.36%
85+	454,877	1,194	3,371	1,878	.26%	.74%	.41%
TOTAL	8,112,544	17,997	45,644	30,663	.22%	.56%	.38%

Movers from other regions: Percent from other regions:

1975-80:	Persons	Northeast	South	West	Northeast	South	West
60-64	2,625,156	5,720	13,568	11,983	.22%	.52%	.46%
65-69	2,244,912	4,558	12,450	10,292	.20%	.55%	.46%
70-74	1,771,637	4,070	10,989	7,180	.23%	.62%	.41%
75+	2,754,443	6,989	22,352	11,592	.25%	.81%	.42%
TOTAL	9,396,148	21,337	59,359	41,047	.23%	.63%	.44%

Source: 1960 to 1980 Censuses of Population

203

A-7
Migration Flows between Regions, by Age, South, 1955-1960, 1965-1970,
and 1975-1980

1955-60:	Movers from other regions:				Percent from other regions:		
	Persons	Northeast	Midwest	West	Northeast	Midwest	West
60-64	1,950,299	35,359	34,854	7,754	1.81%	1.79%	.40%
65-69	1,728,354	42,907	40,145	6,776	2.48%	2.32%	.39%
70-74	1,278,432	25,421	24,402	4,525	1.99%	1.91%	.35%
75+	1,476,397	18,436	17,827	4,125	1.25%	1.21%	.28%
75-79	826,005	11,344	10,744	2,393	1.37%	1.30%	.29%
80-84	411,747	4,767	4,698	1,153	1.16%	1.14%	.28%
85+	238,645	2,325	2,385	579	.97%	1.00%	.24%
TOTAL	6,433,492	122,123	117,228	23,180	1.90%	1.82%	.36%

Movers from other regions: | | | | Percent from other regions:

1965-70:	Persons	Northeast	Midwest	West	Northeast	Midwest	West
60-64	2,664,402	47,342	47,079	13,377	1.78%	1.77%	.50%
65-69	2,204,549	55,075	48,998	9,782	2.50%	2.22%	.44%
70-74	1,645,822	33,534	27,381	6,342	2.04%	1.66%	.39%
75+	2,204,115	28,623	26,390	7,238	1.30%	1.20%	.33%
75-79	1,124,267	16,746	14,208	3,670	1.49%	1.26%	.33%
80-84	644,851	7,285	7,406	2,103	1.13%	1.15%	.33%
85+	434,997	4,592	4,766	1,465	1.06%	1.10%	.34%
TOTAL	9,718,888	164,574	149,839	36,739	1.89%	1.72%	.42%

Movers from other regions: | | | | Percent from other regions:

1975-80:	Persons	Northeast	Midwest	West	Northeast	Midwest	West
60-64	3,327,513	96,429	78,491	22,050	2.90%	2.36%	.66%
65-69	3,014,399	98,051	71,356	18,957	3.25%	2.37%	.63%
70-74	2,360,625	54,909	38,309	11,455	2.33%	1.62%	.49%
75+	3,190,770	52,950	38,417	13,238	1.66%	1.20%	.41%
TOTAL	11,893,307	302,339	226,572	65,600	2.54%	1.91%	.55%

Source: 1960 to 1980 Censuses of Population

A-8
Migration Flows between Regions, by Age, West, 1955-1960, 1965-1970, and 1975-1980

1955-60:	Movers from other regions:				Percent from other regions:		
	Persons	Northeast	Midwest	South	Northeast	Midwest	South
60-64	1,007,379	10,570	26,579	11,220	1.05%	2.64%	1.11%
65-69	876,354	9,857	27,503	8,465	1.12%	3.14%	.97%
70-74	687,489	6,609	18,232	5,649	.96%	2.65%	.82%
75+	795,026	5,483	17,037	6,160	.69%	2.14%	.77%
75-79	444,510	3,359	10,060	3,505	.76%	2.26%	.79%
80-84	226,108	1,414	4,405	1,670	.63%	1.95%	.74%
85+	124,408	710	2,572	985	.57%	2.07%	.79%
TOTAL	3,366,246	32,519	89,351	31,494	.97%	2.65%	.94%

	Movers from other regions:				Percent from other regions:		
1965-70:	Persons	Northeast	Midwest	South	Northeast	Midwest	South
60-64	1,345,442	10,299	20,340	9,603	.77%	1.73%	.71%
65-69	1,071,149	10,130	23,928	8,170	.95%	2.23%	.76%
70-74	830,945	6,974	16,130	5,775	.83%	1.94%	.69%
75+	1,200,392	7,798	20,414	8,306	.65%	1.70%	.69%
75-79	594,276	4,157	10,015	4,059	.70%	1.69%	.68%
80-84	363,245	2,240	6,202	2,375	.62%	1.71%	.65%
85+	242,861	1,401	4,197	1,872	.58%	1.73%	.77%
TOTAL	4,447,917	35,100	93,812	31,854	.79%	1.88%	.72%

	Movers from other regions:				Percent from other regions:		
1975-80:	Persons	Northeast	Midwest	South	Northeast	Midwest	South
60-64	1,809,024	19,909	36,965	17,287	1.10%	2.04%	.96%
65-69	1,526,042	18,549	30,694	14,093	1.22%	2.21%	.92%
70-74	1,159,009	10,635	20,331	9,929	.92%	1.75%	.96%
75+	1,658,399	13,265	28,337	15,048	.80%	1.71%	.91%
TOTAL	6,151,463	62,258	119,327	56,357	1.01%	1.94%	.92%

Source: 1960 to 1980 Censuses of Population

A-9
Indicators of Labor Force Participation by Age, Gender, and Educational Attainment,
United States, 1980

	Total	0-7 yrs	8 yrs	9-11 yrs	12 yrs	13-15 yrs	16+ yrs
MALE 55-59							
Total (000s)	5,499	704	534	1,014	1,710	664	871
Percent:							
with earnings	83.6%	68.8%	78.7%	81.5%	86.4%	87.8%	92.5%
working 35+ hours	77.4%	61.3%	72.2%	75.4%	80.8%	81.5%	86.3%
working 40+ weeks	70.4%	52.2%	63.7%	67.8%	74.4%	75.5%	80.5%
MALE 60-64							
Total (000s)	4,695	729	595	891	1,384	514	592
Percent:							
with earnings	69.8%	55.7%	64.9%	67.4%	73.2%	76.0%	82.8%
working 35+ hours	60.5%	46.8%	53.8%	58.4%	64.1%	66.1%	72.0%
working 40+ weeks	51.6%	37.3%	45.9%	49.0%	55.4%	59.2%	64.7%
MALE 65+							
Total (000s)	10,263	2,698	2,004	1,739	1,964	847	1,011
Percent:							
with earnings	28.7%	19.7%	24.5%	28.5%	33.4%	39.0%	44.3%
working 35+ hours	14.7%	9.5%	11.6%	14.4%	18.1%	20.1%	24.0%
working 40+ weeks	10.0%	5.6%	7.0%	9.4%	12.7%	14.9%	19.1%

Total (000s)	6,154	644	541	1,224	2,466	773	505
Percent:							
with earnings	51.7%	35.7%	42.3%	47.1%	54.6%	59.2%	67.9%
working 35+ hours	37.5%	25.1%	30.0%	33.9%	39.8%	43.2%	50.4%
working 40+ weeks	31.6%	19.7%	24.5%	28.5%	34.6%	37.5%	38.1%

FEMALE 60-64

Total (000s)	5,440	710	666	1,138	1,920	579	427
Percent:							
with earnings	39.8%	27.4%	33.0%	36.9%	42.8%	48.1%	53.9%
working 35+ hours	26.7%	17.3%	20.8%	24.2%	29.2%	33.3%	37.5%
working 40+ weeks	21.4%	13.0%	16.2%	19.5%	24.5%	27.9%	26.0%

FEMALE 65+

Total (000s)	15,236	3,399	2,969	2,784	3,510	1,470	1,103
Percent:							
with earnings	12.3%	7.2%	9.3%	12.6%	15.3%	17.3%	19.6%
working 35+ hours	4.7%	2.5%	3.1%	4.7%	6.4%	6.9%	7.7%
working 40+ weeks	3.2%	1.6%	2.1%	3.1%	4.6%	4.8%	4.8%

Source: 1980 Census of Population

REFERENCES

Burkhauser, R., K. Holden, and D. Feaster. 1988. "Incidence, Timing, and Events Associated with Poverty: A Dynamic View of Poverty in Retirement." *Journal of Gerontology: Social Sciences* 43: S46-52.

Cafferata, G. 1987. "Marital Status, Living Arrangements, and the Use of Health Services by Elderly Persons." *Journal of Gerontology* 42: 613-18.

Chen, Y., and R. Scholen, eds. 1980. *Unlocking Home Equity for the Elderly*. Cambridge, England: Ballinger.

Clark, R., and J. Spengler. 1980. *The Economics of Individual and Population Aging*. Cambridge, England: Cambridge University Press.

Coale, A. 1972. *The Growth and Structure of Human Populations: A Mathematical Investigation*. Princeton, N.J.: Princeton University Press.

Coale, A., and N. Rives. 1973. "A Statistical Reconstruction of the Black Population of the United States 1880-1970." *Population Index* 39: 3-35.

Replacement Fertility in Industrial Societies: Causes, Consequences, Policies. New York: The Population Council. (A supplement to *Population and Development Review*.)

Davis, K. M. Bernstam, and R. Ricardo-Campbell, eds. 1986. *Below Replacement Fertility in Industrial Societies: Causes, Consequences, Policies*. New York: The Population Council. (A supplement to *Population and Development Review*.)

Fay, R., J. Passel, and J. Robinson. 1988. *The Coverage of Population in the 1980 Census.* Washington, D.C.: U.S. Bureau of the Census. PHC80-E4.

Fingerhut, L. 1984. *Changes in Mortality among the Elderly: United States, 1940-78. Supplement to 1980.* Vital and Health Statistics, Series 3, no. 22a. Hyattsville, Md.: U.S. National Center for Health Statistics.

Griffith, J. 1985. *How Older Americans Live.* Washington, D.C.: U.S. Senate Special Committee on Aging.

The Hay Group. 1988. *Social Security Summary 1988.* Philadelphia: Hay/Huggins.

Keyfitz, N. 1968. "Changing Vital Rates and Age Distribution." *Population Studies* 22: 235-51.

Kotlikoff, L., and D. Smith. 1983. *Pensions in the American Economy.* Chicago: University of Chicago Press.

Litwak, E., and C. Longino. 1987. "Migration Patterns among the Elderly: A Developmental Perspective." *The Gerontologist* 27: 266-72.

Manton, K., and G. Myers. 1987. "Recent Trends in Multiple-Cause Mortality 1968 to 1982: Age and Cohort Components." *Population Research and Policy Review* 6: 161-76.

Manton, K., and B. Soldo. 1985. "Dynamics of Health Changes in the Oldest Old: New Perspectives and Evidence." *Milbank Memorial Fund Quarterly* 63: 206-85.

Manton, K., and E. Stallard. 1984. *Recent Trends in Mortality Analysis.* Orlando, Fla.: Academic Press.

Nam, C., N. Weatherby, and K. Ockay. 1978. "Causes of Death Which Contribute to the Mortality Crossover Effect." *Social Biology* 25: 306-14.

Preston, S. 1984. "Children and the Elderly: Divergent Paths for America's Dependents." *Demography* 21: 435-57.

Rabin, D. 1985. "Waxing of the Gray, Waning of the Green." In *Health in an Older Society,* Committee on an Aging Society, ed., 28-56. Washington, D.C.: National Academy Press.

Rogers, A. and L. Castro. 1981. *Model Migration Schedules.* Laxenburg, Austria: International Institute for Applied Systems Analysis.

Rosenstein, M., R. Manderscheid, L. Milazzo-Sayre, and R. MacAskill. 1987. "Patient Characteristics of Elderly Persons Who Receive Mental Health Services." In *Proceedings of the 1987 Public Health Conference on Records and Statistics,* 92. Hyattsville, Md.: U.S. National Center for Health Statistics.

Serow, W. 1975. "The Economics of Stationary and Declining Populations: Some Views from the First Half of the Twentieth Century."

In *Zero Population Growth: Implications*, J. Spengler, ed., 18-33. Chapel Hill, N.C.: Carolina Population Center.

Serow, W. 1982. "Changes in the Composition of the Elderly Poor: 1969 to 1978." *The Journal of Applied Social Sciences* 7: 57-68.

Serow, W. 1984. "The Impact of Population Change on Consumption." In *Economic Consequences of Population Change in Industrialized Countries*, G. Steinmann, ed., 168-78. Berlin: Springer-Verlag.

Serow, W., and D. Charity. 1988. "Return Migration of the Elderly in the United States: Recent Trends." *Research on Aging* 10: 155-68.

Siegel, J. 1974. "Estimates of Coverage of the Population by Sex, Race, and Age in the 1970 Census." *Demography* 11: 1-24.

Smeeding, T. 1982. *Alternative Methods for Valuing Selected In-Kind Transfer Benefits and Measuring Their Effect on Poverty.* Technical Paper no. 50. Washington, D.C.: U.S. Bureau of the Census.

Spencer, G. 1984. *Projections of the Population of the United States by Age, Sex and Race: 1983 to 2080.* Current Population Reports. Series P-25, no. 952. Washington, D.C.: U.S. Bureau of the Census.

Spencer, G. 1989. *Projections of the Population of the United States by Age, Sex and Race: 1988 to 2080.* Current Population Reports. Series P-25, no. 1018. Washington, D.C.: U.S. Bureau of the Census.

Taeuber, I., and C. Taeuber. 1971. *People of the United States in the 20th Century.* Washington, D.C.: U.S. Bureau of the Census.

Teitelbaum, M., and J. Winter. 1985. *The Fear of Population Decline.* Orlando, Fla.: Academic Press.

Torrey, B. 1985. "Sharing Increasing Costs on Declining Income: The Visible Dilemma of the Invisible Aged." *Milbank Memorial Fund Quarterly* 63: 377-94.

Torrey, B., K. Kinsella, and C. Taeuber. 1987. *An Aging World.* International Population Reports. Series P-95, no. 78. Washington, D.C.: U.S. Bureau of the Census.

U.S. Bureau of the Census. 1977. *Projections of the Population of the United States by Age, Sex and Race: 1977 to 2050.* Current Population Reports. Series P-25, no. 704. Washington, D.C.: U.S. Bureau of the Census.

U.S. Bureau of the Census. 1982. *1980 Census of Population: General Population Characteristics.* Washington, D.C.: U.S. Bureau of the Census.

U.S. Bureau of the Census. 1986. *Household Wealth and Asset Ownership: 1984.* Household Economic Studies. Series P-70, no. 7. Washington, D.C.: U.S. Bureau of the Census.

U.S. Bureau of the Census. 1987. *Geographic Mobility: 1985.* Current Population Reports. Series P-20, no. 420. Washington, D.C.: U.S. Bureau of the Census.

U.S. Bureau of the Census. 1988a. *Household and Family Characteristics.* Current Population Reports. Series P-20, no. 424. Washington, D.C.: U.S. Government Printing Office.

U.S. Bureau of the Census. 1988b. *Marital Status and Living Arrangements: March 1987.* Current Population Reports. Series P-20, no. 423. Washington, D.C.: U.S. Bureau of the Census.

U.S. Bureau of the Census. 1988c. *State Population and Household Estimates with Age, Sex and Components of Change: 1981 to 1987.* Current Population Reports. Series P-25, no. 1024. Washington, D.C.: U.S. Bureau of the Census.

U.S. Bureau of the Census. 1988d. *United States Population Estimates by Age, Sex and Race: 1980 to 1987.* Current Population Reports. Series P-25, no. 1027. Washington, D.C.: U.S. Bureau of the Census.

U.S. Bureau of the Census. 1989a. *Money Income of Households, Families and Persons in the United States: 1987.* Current Population Reports. Series P-60, no. 162. Washington, D.C.: U.S. Government Printing Office.

U.S. Bureau of the Census. 1989b. *Poverty in the United States: 1987.* Current Population Reports. Series P-60, no. 163. Washington, D.C.: Government Printing Office.

U.S. Bureau of Labor Statistics. September 24, 1987. "Consumer Expenditure Survey Results from 1985." *U.S. Department of Labor News.*

U.S. National Center for Health Statistics. 1984. *Health Characteristics According to Family and Personal Income.* Vital and Health Statistics. Series 10, no. 147. Hyattsville, Md.: U.S. National Center for Health Statistics.

U.S. National Center for Health Statistics. 1986. *Vital Statistics of the United States, 1982. Part 2, Mortality.* Hyattsville, Md.: U.S. National Center for Health Statistics.

U.S. National Center for Health Statistics. 1987a. "Advance Report on Final Mortality Statistics, 1985." *Monthly Vital Statistics Report.* Vol. 36, no. 5, supplement. Hyattsville, Md.: U.S. National Center for Health Statistics.

U.S. National Center for Health Statistics, 1987b. *Health Statistics on Older Persons, 1986.* Analytical and Epidemiological Studies. Series 3, no. 25. Hyattsville, Md.: U.S. National Center for Health Statistics.

U.S. National Center for Health Statistics, 1988. *Vital Statistics of the United States, 1986.* Life Tables. Vol. 2, Section 6. Hyattsville, Md.: U.S. National Center for Health Statistics.

U.S. Senate, Special Committee on Aging. 1988. *Aging America: Trends and Projections.* Washington, D.C.: U.S. Government Printing Office.

van den Boomen, J. 1981. "Age-Cost Profiles: A Common Denominator?"
    In *International Population Conference: Solicited Papers,* Vol. 3,
    285-99. Liege, Belgium: International Union for the Scientific
    Study of Population.
Verbrugge, L. 1979. "Marital Status and Health." *Journal of Marriage
    and the Family* 41: 267-85.

INDEX

220 Index

"Statistical Reconstruction of the
  Black Population of the United
  States 1880-1970" (Coale and
  Rives), 23
Survey of Income and Program
  Participation, 119

Taeuber, C., 1, 43, 193, 195, 213
Taeuber, I., 43, 213
Teitelbaum, M., 184, 213
Torrey, B., 1, 142, 182, 193, 195,
  213

United States: Bureau of the
  Census, 2, 5, 9, 13, 17, 21, 35,
  38, 47, 53, 55, 59, 60, 63, 67,
  69, 73, 76, 81, 85, 88, 90, 92,
  93, 96, 97, 105, 107, 112, 114,
  117, 119, 121, 126, 201, 203,
  205, 207, 209, 213; Bureau of
  Labor Statistics, 122, 214;
  National Center for Health Statistics, 21, 25, 28, 32, 40, 129,
  131, 133, 135, 136, 137, 138,

140, 142, 145, 150, 153, 157,
158, 160, 162, 166, 168, 170,
173, 175, 177, 183, 214; Office
of Management and Budget,
113; Senate, 101, 102, 214
*Unlocking Home Equity for the
Elderly* (Chen and Spengler),
93

van den Boomen, J., 184, 215
Verbrugge, L., 215
*Vital Statistics of the United
States, 1982* (U.S. National
Center for Health Statistics),
21
*Vital Statistics of the United
States, 1986* (U.S. National
Center for Health Statistics),
25, 40, 140, 183

"Waxing of the Gray, Waning of
the Green" (Rabin), 142, 179
Weatherby, N., 23, 212
Winter, J., 184, 213

About the Authors

WILLIAM J. SEROW is Associate Director of the Center for the Study of Population and Professor of Economics at Florida State University. He is the author of many articles and books on topics relating to migration, small area demography, population economics, and the demographic and economic aspects of aging.

DAVID F. SLY is Director of the Center for the Study of Population and Professor of Sociology at Florida State University. He is the author of many articles and books on topics relating to migration, urbanization, human ecology, and the demographic and social aspects of aging.

J. MICHAEL WRIGLEY has been a Postdoctoral Fellow at the Center for Demographic Studies at Duke University since 1988. He is the author of several articles on health and mortality, migration, and human ecology.